Introduction

"**I** love reading poetry with my students, but I just don't know how to teach them to read a poem and respond to it." Are you one of countless teachers who share this sentiment? If so, the simple, structured lessons of *Read and Understand Poetry* are just what you need!

- Easy-to-follow lessons guide you in introducing and reading poems chosen especially for students at your grade level.

- Quick and easy minilessons help you work with your students on the language arts skills that are unique to poetry.

- Individual follow-up activity pages help students consolidate what they have learned and extend their critical thinking and creativity.

What's on the Teacher Page?

The **teacher page** provides a simple, easy-to-follow lesson plan that includes these features:

The **Before You Read** section provides important background information for you to share with students prior to reading the poem. Guidelines for developing key concepts and suggestions for preteaching vocabulary are found here.

The **While You Read** section helps you choose the best way for students to experience each poem for the first time (such as listening to you read it aloud, reading it aloud chorally or individually, reading it silently, etc.).

The **After You Read** section guides you in presenting minilessons that focus on different types of poetry and on important elements of the language arts curriculum for poetry.

What's on the Poem Page?

Each **poem page** presents:

- the text of the poetry featured in the lesson

- a simple illustration to enhance comprehension

- the "Did You Know?" feature appears on some poem pages to present interesting information about the poet or the poem

snowflakes
slip from the sky
like soft white butterflies

What's on the Follow-up Activity Pages?

As you guide students through the lessons outlined on the Teacher Page, they will have multiple opportunities to work as part of a group on developing an understanding of the form and content of each poem. The Follow-up Activities give students the opportunity to synthesize new information and practice language arts skills introduced during teacher-directed minilessons.

The first page of **Follow-up Activities** is designed to help students consolidate their comprehension of the poem by having them select the only correct response out of four possible choices for each of these multiple-choice items. Item content covers:

- literal comprehension
- sequence
- word meanings
- context clues and inferences
- main idea and details

In addition, the item format on this first activity page emulates the format students are likely to encounter on standardized language arts tests. After completing the activity pages in *Read and Understand Poetry*, students will be undaunted when a poem is presented as a reading passage on their next standardized test.

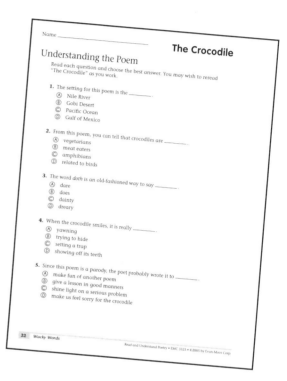

The second page of **Follow-up Activities** may focus on any aspect of the language arts curriculum touched upon in the poem. Students may be invited to share their opinions as they respond to open-ended questions, to try their hand at using poetic techniques such as onomatopoeia or alliteration, or to write a poem of their own. Critical thinking and creativity are encouraged on this type of activity page.

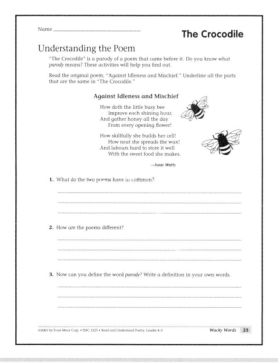

What Are the Additional Student Resources?

A six-page **Glossary of Poetry Terms** features kid-friendly definitions and pronunciation guidelines for terms ranging from *alliteration* to *simile*. Each glossary entry includes an example drawn from this anthology, further strengthening students' connection to poetry terminology.

An **About the Poets** feature presents brief, high-interest information on each of the poets included in this anthology. This helps build the additional context that allows students to deepen their understanding of the work of specific poets.

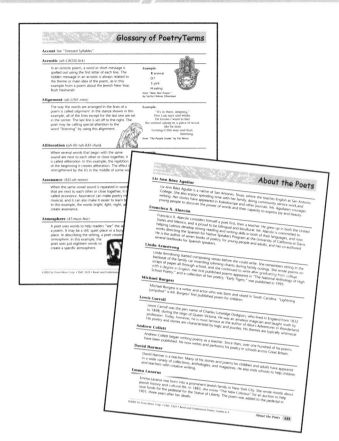

How to Use These Materials

To create a unique poetry anthology for your students, reproduce for each student:

- the cover page for the student *Read & Understand Poetry Anthology*
- the table of contents for each unit
- the poem and follow-up activity pages for each poem
- the Glossary of Poetry Terms and About the Poets pages

Place these pages together in a folder or three-ring binder to create individual poetry anthologies.

As students encounter new poems in their ongoing reading, they can use this resource to help them enjoy and deepen their knowledge of this timeless art form.

Family Album

Contents

Before You Read the Poem

Build Background

To help prepare students to read the poem, ask: *What do mothers do for their children? How do mothers take care of us? What do we do with our mothers for fun?* Record students' responses on a word web. Possible responses include: *cook food, tell stories, play games, take pictures,* etc.

Build Vocabulary

Tell students that there is a Spanish phrase in this poem. It is "canción verde," which means "green song." If you have Spanish-speaking students in class, invite a volunteer to translate the phrase for the class. Otherwise, write the phrase and its English equivalent on the board. Then ask students: *How can a song be green? What does the phrase "green song" make you see or feel?*

While You Read the Poem

Read the poem aloud for the class. Model the pronunciation of the Spanish words: In *canción*: the first *c* is hard, the second *c* is soft, and the accent is on the last syllable; the *r* in *verde* is slightly rolled. There are several instances in which a comma appears in the middle of a line; model how to pause at these commas. When you are finished, invite volunteers to take turns reading the poem aloud.

After You Read the Poem

Elements of Poetry

Form: Free Verse This poem is written as free verse. That means there are no rhyming words and no established rhythm. Nevertheless, it still has a poetic quality. With students, talk about the different elements that make this "sound like a poem," even though there are no rhymes or rhythm. Students might notice that the poem is made up of four sentences. Each sentence is broken up into smaller phrases, separated by commas. These phrases evoke the sights, sounds, smells, and sensations of an intimate scene at home.

Poet's Toolbox: Metaphor and Simile Explain to students that poets use similes and metaphors to compare things. The comparisons help us to visualize or feel something that cannot usually be touched or seen. In a metaphor, one thing is described as if it were something else; for example: "Your laugh is a green song." A simile uses the word *like* or *as*. The identification is not quite as strong as a metaphor, for example: "Your laugh is *like* a green song." Write these examples on the board to help explain the difference between metaphors and similes. Students will have more practice on the second activity page.

Follow-up Activities

Students may work independently to complete the activities on pages 8 and 9.

Song to Mothers

1 Your laugh is a green song,

2 canción verde,

3 that branches

4 through our house,

5 its yellow blooms smelling

6 like warm honey.

7 Your laugh peels apples

8 and stirs their cinnamon bubblings,

9 then opens a book and pulls me

10 onto your lap.

11 At night, your laugh kisses

12 us soft as a petal, smooths my pillow

13 and covers me, a soft leafy blanket,

14 green and yellow.

15 I snuggle into your laugh,

16 your canción verde

17 and dream of growing

18 into my own green song.

—*Pat Mora*

Understanding the Poem

Read each question and choose the best answer. You may wish to reread "Song to Mothers" as you work.

1. The narrator of the poem is probably _____.

   Ⓐ a mother
   Ⓑ a teenager
   Ⓒ a small child
   Ⓓ a full-grown adult

2. The poem is about the _____ of the narrator's mother.

   Ⓐ smile
   Ⓑ laughter
   Ⓒ special dishes
   Ⓓ favorite songs

3. You can tell that the narrator _____.

   Ⓐ barely speaks English
   Ⓑ doesn't know how to talk yet
   Ⓒ speaks another language besides English
   Ⓓ is fluent in at least three different languages

4. You can tell that the narrator's mother _____.

   Ⓐ doesn't like to read
   Ⓑ likes to brush her hair
   Ⓒ wishes she didn't have to work
   Ⓓ spends a lot of time with her children

5. What could *bubblings* in line 8 mean?

   Ⓐ soap bubbles
   Ⓑ mumbling and laughter
   Ⓒ bubbles in cooking apples
   Ⓓ eating with your mouth full

Name _____

Understanding the Poem

1. Similes and metaphors compare things. When two things are compared, it helps us see what the poet wants us to see. What is *laughter* compared to in the first six lines of the poem?

_____

_____

_____

2. The poet describes laughter as if it can do certain things. When human qualities or actions are attributed to nonhuman things, we call it *personification*. How does the poet use personification to describe laughter in lines 7 through 13?

_____

_____

3. In lines 13 and 14, the poet says that the mother's laughter is "a soft leafy blanket, green and yellow." Is this a metaphor or personification?

_____

4. Write your own metaphor or simile here. Describe the laugh, smile, or voice of someone you know. Compare it to something else to help describe it.

_____

_____

_____

5. Use personification to help describe a laugh, a smile, or the sound of someone's voice. Write a sentence telling what one of these things "does." Can it sweep out a room? Blow away the clouds? Make your heart sing? Be creative!

_____

_____

_____

Before You Read the Poem

Build Background and Vocabulary

This poem is set in the desert of the Southwest. Ask students what they know about this region. Brainstorm the names of plants and animals. Record student responses in a word web like this one:

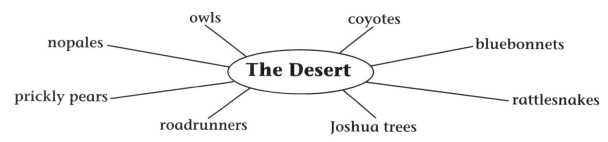

Be sure to include *nopales* (say noh-PAH-less) and *prickly pears*, as shown. Tell students that nopales are a kind of cactus plant. The "flesh" of the nopal is peeled, sliced, and cooked in some southwestern and Mexican dishes. Likewise, the prickly pear is also edible. The inside of this cactus fruit is pink to red in coloring, and it is mildly sweet, but the outside is covered with very thin thorns, hence the name. Invite volunteers who have eaten these foods to share their impressions with the class.

While You Read the Poem

Invite volunteers to take turns reading the poem aloud. If necessary, model the pronunciation of *nopales*.

After You Read the Poem

Elements of Poetry

Form: Stanzas This poem is made up of four stanzas. Explain to students that a stanza is a group of related sentences or phrases. In a sense, a stanza is somewhat like a paragraph. The lines in a stanza are related in the same way that the sentences of a paragraph "go together." Each stanza in this poem focuses on a different part of the scene. Students will identify some of these details on the second activity page.

Poet's Toolbox: Alliteration Alliteration is the repetition of initial sounds. As an example, point out the phrase "prickly pears" in the first stanza. Students will have more practice with alliteration on the second activity page.

Follow-up Activities

Students may work independently to complete the activities on pages 12 and 13.

My Grandma Is Like a Flowering Cactus

1 every fall
   the nopales
   around my house
   and neighborhood
   are laden with prickly pears

2 my grandma
   sings with joy
   when she picks
   the prickly pears
   she knows are
   ripe and sweet

3 tongs and
   knife in hand
   my grandma
   peels prickly pears
   —the delicacies
   of the desert

4 since she knows
   these succulents
   are also my favorite
   fruits by far
   my grandma can't
   stop winking at me

—*Francisco X. Alarcón*

Did You Know? Francisco X. Alarcón is an award-winning author of poetry for both children and adults, written in both English and Spanish. He considers himself "bi-national" because four generations of his family have spent their lives in both the United States and Mexico. When he is not writing poetry, Mr. Alarcón directs a Spanish for Native Speakers program, teaching university students who speak Spanish to also read and write it.

Name _____

Understanding the Poem

Read each question and choose the best answer. You may wish to reread
"My Grandma Is Like a Flowering Cactus" as you work.

1. Prickly pears are ready to eat in the _____ .
   - Ⓐ winter
   - Ⓑ spring
   - Ⓒ autumn
   - Ⓓ summer

2. Grandma uses tongs to handle prickly pears because they are _____ .
   - Ⓐ small
   - Ⓑ slippery
   - Ⓒ too hot to hold
   - Ⓓ covered with thorns

3. "Delicacies" are probably things that are _____ .
   - Ⓐ good to eat
   - Ⓑ soft and silky
   - Ⓒ easy to break
   - Ⓓ rough and dry

4. A *succulent* is probably _____ .
   - Ⓐ a type of step stool
   - Ⓑ a type of cactus fruit
   - Ⓒ a fruit candy to suck on
   - Ⓓ a tool used for grasping

5. The poet probably says that his grandmother is like a flowering cactus
   because she _____ .
   - Ⓐ lives in the desert
   - Ⓑ wears flowers in her hair
   - Ⓒ can hurt him, just like cactus thorns
   - Ⓓ is sweet, just like the fruit of a prickly pear

Read and Understand Poetry • EMC 3325 • ©2005 by Evan-Moor Corp.

Understanding the Poem

1. A stanza is a group of lines in a poem. What is the first stanza in the poem about?

   _____

   What are the second and third stanzas about?

   _____

   How does the poet pull all of these things together in the last stanza?

   _____

2. *Alliteration* is the repetition of a group of consonant sounds. The phrase "The mysterious midnight moon" is an example of alliteration. All the main words start with the letter *m*. What's an example of alliteration in the second stanza?

   _____

   What are two examples of alliteration in the third stanza?

   _____

   _____

   Can you find the alliteration in the last stanza?

   _____

   Now, make up your own alliterations about plants and animals in the desert.

   _____

   _____

   _____

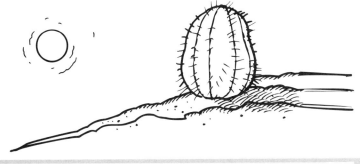

Family Album   **13**

Before You Read the Poem

Build Background

Tell students that this poem is set in the distant past. The time and place aren't specified, but it seems to be in a rural area in a Spanish-speaking place, possibly Mexico or the American Southwest. In the past, women were prohibited from doing "manly" things in the Southwest, in Mexico, and in many other places in the United States and around the world. Ask students to use these clues and the poem's title to predict what this poem is about.

Build Vocabulary

Explain to students that *abuela* is Spanish for "grandmother." You may also want to explain that *caballero* means "cowboy" or "horse-trainer," and that the feminine form of this noun, *caballera,* is used at the end of the poem to make a point. Students will be asked to make an inference about this on the first activity page.

While You Read the Poem

Form groups of students. Have each group chorally read a different stanza. You may want to switch groups a few times so that students have a chance to read different parts of the poem.

After You Read the Poem

Elements of Poetry

Form: Narrative Verse This poem is a narrative—it tells a story. As you read the poem aloud with students, pause at the end of each stanza and have students summarize what has happened. Students will record each event of the "story" on the second activity page.

Poet's Toolbox: Action Verbs A good story is so much more interesting to read if it includes lots of action verbs. That's especially true of stories in verse! This poem has lots of examples of lively action verbs. To illustrate, ask students to hunt for all the verbs that describe how the young woman and her horse move. They should find the following: *galloped, race, swept across,* and *trotted.* These words make it easy to see the action. Ask students to find other action verbs in the poem.

Follow-up Activities

Students may work independently to complete the activities on pages 17 and 18.

The Race

1   She rode a horse named Fina
when women didn't ride.
They galloped around the mountain,
her legs on Fina's side.

2   She let her hair down from its bun
and felt it whip and fly.
She laughed and sang and whooped out loud.
Up there she wasn't shy!

3   One day great-grandma found her out
and planned to stop it all.
But down in town they'd heard some news. . .
they told her of a call.

4   A call for the caballeros
from all the highs and lows
to race their fancy caballos
to try and win the rose.

5   Abuela looked at Fina,
a twinkle in her eye.
Abuela said, "Let's enter!
This race deserves a try."

6 At dawn she was the only girl,
   but didn't even care.
   She came to meet the challenge, and
   her horse was waiting there.

7 They swept across the finish line
   much faster than the rest.
   She flung her hat without surprise;
   she'd always done her best.

8 Fina shook her mane and stomped.
   Abuela flashed a smile.
   She sniffed the rose and trotted off
   in caballera style!

—*Jennifer Trujillo*

Read and Understand Poetry • EMC 3325 • ©2005 by Evan-Moor Corp.

Name _____

Understanding the Poem

Read each question and choose the best answer. You may wish to reread
"The Race" as you work.

1. Who is the woman who won the race?
   - (A) Fina
   - (B) The poem doesn't say.
   - (C) the poet's great-grandmother
   - (D) Abuela, the poet's grandmother

2. *Caballero* is a Spanish word. In this poem, it probably means something
   like _____.
   - (A) driver
   - (B) cowboy
   - (C) veterinarian
   - (D) animal trainer

3. The prize for winning the race was _____.
   - (A) a rose
   - (B) a horse
   - (C) a fancy hat
   - (D) a leather saddle

4. How many women were in the race?
   - (A) a few
   - (B) none
   - (C) one
   - (D) more than a few

5. You can tell that Abuela was probably _____.
   - (A) shy and timid
   - (B) a feisty old horse
   - (C) all talk and no action
   - (D) the first woman to ever win this race

©2005 by Evan-Moor Corp. • EMC 3325 • Read and Understand Poetry   *Family Album*   17

The Race

Understanding the Poem

"The Race" tells a story. Summarize each part of the story in your own words.

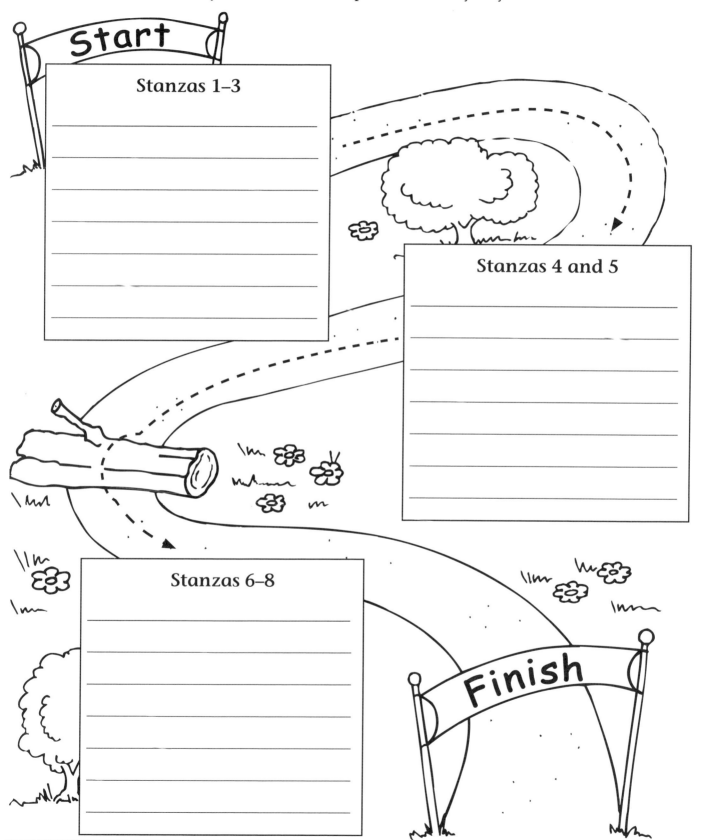

Start

Stanzas 1–3

Stanzas 4 and 5

Stanzas 6–8

Finish

Read and Understand Poetry • EMC 3325 • ©2005 by Evan-Moor Corp.

Wacky Words

Contents

Before You Read the Poem

Build Background

Introduce this unit by telling students that they are going to read three wacky poems that were written strictly for laughs. This particular poem, "The Crocodile," is by Lewis Carroll, a famous author of children's literature. He is perhaps best known for writing *Alice's Adventures in Wonderland* and *Through the Looking-Glass*. Invite students to share what they know about these books. Share with students that Carroll also wrote poetry. The poems of Lewis Carroll are known for being nonsensical. They are fun to read because they are about fantastical characters in absurd situations. Later in this unit, students will have the opportunity to read "Jabberwocky," one of Carroll's most famous poems.

While You Read the Poem

Ask students to study this poem for a few minutes. Then challenge any volunteers to recite the poem from memory. During the recitation, ask other students to check their printed copies to make sure there are no mistakes. Invite another volunteer to try reciting the poem from memory, and so on, until all who would like to have had a chance.

After You Read the Poem

Elements of Poetry

Form: Parody In the 1800s, students were required to memorize lengthy poems that instructed them in proper behavior. Carroll thought these poems were boring and made fun of them in poems like "The Crocodile," which is a parody of an earlier poem entitled "Against Idleness and Mischief." Students will compare these two poems on the second activity page. There they are guided to the conclusion that a parody is an imitation of another work that pokes fun at the original.

Poet's Toolbox: Verb Forms In French and Spanish, the subjunctive tense is commonly used in conversation. Not so in English. In fact, the subjunctive is hardly ever used in English. It is associated with poetry from the nineteenth century and earlier. In the subjunctive, the simple form of the verb is used with the third-person singular; for example: "Fair be the day." Help students find the two subjunctive verbs in the first stanza, which are "How doth the crocodile" and "pour the waters of the Nile." In both of these expressions, *doth* and *pour* are used in conjunction with *crocodile*. A poet today would probably use *does* and *pour*.

Follow-up Activities

Students may work independently to complete the activities on pages 22 and 23.

The Crocodile

How doth the little crocodile
   Improve his shining tail,
And pour the waters of the Nile
   On every golden scale!

How cheerfully he seems to grin!
   How neatly spreads his claws,
And welcomes little fishes in
   With gently smiling jaws!

—*Lewis Carroll*

 Did You Know? Lewis Carroll was shy as a child and was very nervous when he spoke to adults. He always preferred the company of children, even after he grew up. He enjoyed making up games, riddles, and puzzles for his "little friends."

Understanding the Poem

Read each question and choose the best answer. You may wish to reread "The Crocodile" as you work.

1. The setting for this poem is the _____.
   - Ⓐ Nile River
   - Ⓑ Gobi Desert
   - Ⓒ Pacific Ocean
   - Ⓓ Gulf of Mexico

2. From this poem, you can tell that crocodiles are _____.
   - Ⓐ vegetarians
   - Ⓑ meat eaters
   - Ⓒ amphibians
   - Ⓓ related to birds

3. The word *doth* is an old-fashioned way to say _____.
   - Ⓐ dare
   - Ⓑ does
   - Ⓒ dainty
   - Ⓓ dreary

4. When the crocodile smiles, it is really _____.
   - Ⓐ yawning
   - Ⓑ trying to hide
   - Ⓒ setting a trap
   - Ⓓ showing off its teeth

5. Since this poem is a parody, the poet probably wrote it to _____.
   - Ⓐ make fun of another poem
   - Ⓑ give a lesson in good manners
   - Ⓒ shine light on a serious problem
   - Ⓓ make us feel sorry for the crocodile

Read and Understand Poetry • EMC 3325 • ©2005 by Evan-Moor Corp.

The Crocodile

Understanding the Poem

"The Crocodile" is a parody of a poem that came before it. Do you know what *parody* means? These activities will help you find out.

Read the original poem, "Against Idleness and Mischief." Underline all the parts that are the same in "The Crocodile."

Against Idleness and Mischief

How doth the little busy bee
    Improve each shining hour,
And gather honey all the day
    From every opening flower!

How skillfully she builds her cell!
    How neat she spreads the wax!
And labours hard to store it well
    With the sweet food she makes.

—*Isaac Watts*

1. What do the two poems have in common?

_____

_____

_____

2. How are the poems different?

_____

_____

_____

3. Now can you define the word *parody*? Write a definition in your own words.

_____

_____

_____

Before You Read the Poems

Build Background

The poems students are about to read are from *The Book of Nonsense* by Edward Lear. There are 112 numbered poems in *The Book of Nonsense*, and they are all limericks. This poetic form is at least one hundred years old, and it may be much older. *The Book of Nonsense*, published in 1846, is one of the first printed volumes of limericks. In fact, Edward Lear is regarded as the author who, more than any other, helped to popularize limericks in the late 1800s. Limericks grew in popularity at the turn of the twentieth century, when newspapers held limerick contests, with big prizes offered to the best and the funniest. Limericks have continued to be a popular source of humor ever since. They are often used to tell jokes. Tell students that the three poems they are about to read (numbers 15, 65, and 112 from the collection) are each like a joke with a punch line. They will have to "read between the lines" to get the jokes.

While You Read the Poems

Many limericks are based on an oral tradition and are told from memory. To help students appreciate the oral aspect of limericks, tell them that you are going to hold a limerick contest. Tell students to choose one of the limericks and memorize it. They will probably need to practice saying the poem aloud for at least ten minutes. Then invite students to take turns reciting the poems for the class. You may want to conduct votes to award prizes in different categories: best memory, best delivery, etc.

After You Read the Poems

Elements of Poetry

Form: Limerick Generally speaking, a limerick follows an *aabba* rhyming pattern. Lines 1, 2, and 5 have eight or nine syllables. Lines 3 and 4 have fewer syllables than the rest of the poem—anywhere from five to seven syllables—although lines 3 and 4 should both have the same number of syllables.

Poet's Toolbox: Capitalization Point out that the "names" of the characters in these poems have been capitalized. They aren't really names per se, they're just descriptions of who the characters are or where they come from, for example, Old Man of the Dee; Young Lady of Clare. By capitalizing these descriptive phrases, the poet raises the phrase to the level of an official title or name. Ask students why they think Lear might have done this. The names of these characters aren't known or important, so Lear could call them anything handy or convenient. Also, it's easier to make a rhyme with phrases than with people's names. Most likely, Lear was accentuating the nonsensical nature of these poems by giving official-sounding titles to absurd characters.

Follow-up Activities

Students may work independently to complete the activities on pages 26 and 27.

Selections from
The Book of Nonsense

15.
There was an Old Man in a boat,
Who said, "I'm afloat! I'm afloat!"
When they said, "No! you ain't!"
He was ready to faint,
That unhappy Old Man in a boat.

65.
There was an Old Man of the Dee
Who was sadly annoyed by a flea;
When he said, "I will scratch it,"
They gave him a hatchet,
Which grieved that Old Man of the Dee.

112.
There was a Young Lady of Clare,
Who was sadly pursued by a bear;
When she found she was tired,
She abruptly expired
That unfortunate Lady of Clare.

—Edward Lear

Name _____

Understanding the Poems

Read each question and choose the best answer. You may wish to reread
"Selections from *The Book of Nonsense*" as you work.

1. These poems are meant to make the reader _____.
   - Ⓐ think about a problem
   - Ⓑ giggle at something silly
   - Ⓒ feel what other people feel
   - Ⓓ marvel at the wonders of nature

2. The Old Man in a boat was ready to faint because he _____.
   - Ⓐ was afloat
   - Ⓑ was sinking
   - Ⓒ only had one oar
   - Ⓓ couldn't understand what anybody was saying

3. Why was the Old Man of the Dee "grieved"?
   - Ⓐ He was bothered by a flea.
   - Ⓑ He hurt himself with the hatchet.
   - Ⓒ He felt badly about hurting the flea.
   - Ⓓ He couldn't use a hatchet to scratch himself.

4. In limerick 112, what does "abruptly expired" mean?
   - Ⓐ suddenly died
   - Ⓑ rudely awakened
   - Ⓒ became hopelessly lost
   - Ⓓ stopped without any warning

5. What probably happened to the Lady of Clare?
   - Ⓐ She caught the bear.
   - Ⓑ She cried all the way home.
   - Ⓒ She was caught by the bear.
   - Ⓓ She rested, then ran on some more.

Understanding the Poems

1. All limericks follow the same basic pattern. Reread this poem from *The Book of Nonsense.* Underline all the parts of this poem that are identical to the other two poems:

There was an Old Man in a boat,   _____

Who said, "I'm afloat! I'm afloat!"   _____

When they said, "No! you ain't!"   _____

He was ready to faint,   _____

That unhappy Old Man in a boat.   _____

2. Find the rhyming pattern for this limerick. On the lines above, write *a* next to the lines that end with the same rhyming sound, and *b* next to the lines that end with a different rhyming sound. One pattern might be *abbba.* Write the pattern you find here:

_____

3. Write your own limerick below. First, think of a person and where he or she is from. The person doesn't have to be real—the crazier the better! Then make up a funny situation. Write your limerick using the same rhyming pattern as the poems in *The Book of Nonsense.*

_____

_____

_____

_____

_____

_____

_____

Before You Read the Poem

Build Background

Tell students that the poem they are about to read is by Lewis Carroll, the same poet who wrote "The Crocodile," which they read earlier in this unit. "Jabberwocky" is from Carroll's world-famous book, *Through the Looking-Glass*. Specifically, it appears in the chapter called "Humpty Dumpty." Students may refer to that chapter of the book if they would like to learn more about the Jabberwock. Otherwise, you can simply tell them that the Jabberwock is a kind of dragon. The poem tells the story of a deadly battle between the Jabberwock and a courageous young boy.

While You Read the Poem

This poem is fun to read aloud because of all the invented words in it. For the same reason, some of the words can be challenging to pronounce! Model how to pronounce invented words such as *gimble*, which probably starts with a hard /g/, but use your own judgment for these and any other made-up words. Only Lewis himself knew how the words were meant to be pronounced. Then form groups of students and have each group read one of the stanzas aloud.

After You Read the Poem

Elements of Poetry

Form: Rhyming Verse "Jabberwocky" is a poem in rhyming verse. Ask students to help you identify the rhyming pattern of stanzas 1, 2, 4, and 7, which is *abab*. Then direct their attention to stanzas 3, 5, and 6. The rhyming pattern in those stanzas is *abcb*. In the *c* line, Carroll makes up for the "missing rhyme" by creating rhymes within the line itself. In the third stanza, for example, the *c* line reads: "So rested he by the Tumtum tree." Since *he* rhymes with *tree*, we don't notice that the end of the *c* line doesn't rhyme with the end of the *a* line, a pattern established by the two previous stanzas.

Poet's Toolbox: Invented Words Virtually every other word in this poem has been invented by the author. You won't find these words in a dictionary, but you can guess what a lot of them might mean. Carroll has cleverly taken advantage of traditional settings, actions, and imagery to help suggest possible interpretations for this otherwise nonsensical poem. For example, we don't know what *brillig* means, but it probably has something to do with the weather, and other clues in the stanza suggest that the setting is probably dark and swampy. Talk about the other invented words with students. They will look at these words more closely on the second activity page.

Follow-up Activities

Students may work independently to complete the activities on pages 30 and 31.

Jabberwocky

1 'Twas brillig, and the slithy toves
   Did gyre and gimble in the wabe:
   All mimsy were the borogoves
   And the mome raths outgrabe.

2 "Beware the Jabberwock, my son!
   The jaws that bite, the claws that catch!
   Beware the Jubjub bird, and shun
   The frumious Bandersnatch!"

3 He took his vorpal sword in hand:
   Long time the manxome foe he sought—
   So rested he by the Tumtum tree,
   And stood awhile in thought.

4 And, as in uffish thought he stood,
   The Jabberwock, with eyes of flame,
   Came whiffling through the tulgey wood,
   And burbled as it came!

5 One, two! One, two! And through and through
   The vorpal blade went snicker-snack!
   He left it dead, and with its head
   He went galumphing back.

6 "And hast thou slain the Jabberwock?
   Come to my arms, my beamish boy!
   O frabjous day! Callooh! Callay!"
   He chortled in his joy.

7 'Twas brillig, and the slithy toves
   Did gyre and gimble in the wabe;
   All mimsy were the borogoves,
   And the mome raths outgrabe.

—*Lewis Carroll*

Jabberwocky

Understanding the Poem

Read each question and choose the best answer. You may wish to reread "Jabberwocky" as you work.

1. The Jabberwock appears to be _____.
   - Ⓐ a wise old man
   - Ⓑ a horrible monster
   - Ⓒ a helpless little boy
   - Ⓓ a graceful, long-necked bird

2. The _____ probably has feathers and a beak.
   - Ⓐ Jubjub
   - Ⓑ Tumtum
   - Ⓒ Jabberwock
   - Ⓓ Bandersnatch

3. The deadly battle took place in front of the _____.
   - Ⓐ slithy toves
   - Ⓑ borogoves
   - Ⓒ Tumtum tree
   - Ⓓ frumious Bandersnatch

4. "Callooh! Callay!" probably means something like _____.
   - Ⓐ Achoo!
   - Ⓑ Pow! Bam!
   - Ⓒ Hip, hip, hooray!
   - Ⓓ You must be kidding!

5. This poem is probably based on stories about _____.
   - Ⓐ Cinderella
   - Ⓑ knights and dragons
   - Ⓒ the Loch Ness monster
   - Ⓓ the search for hidden treasure

   Read and Understand Poetry • EMC 3325 • ©2005 by Evan-Moor Corp.

Name _____

Jabberwocky

Understanding the Poem

"Jabberwocky" has lots of made-up words. Still, you can almost guess what these words might mean. It helps to first decide whether the word is a noun, an adjective, or a verb. Here are some reminders:

- A **noun** names a person, place, or thing. Examples: *pond, forest, monster, knight*
- A **verb** is an action word. It tells what somebody or something does. Examples: *search, find, destroy*
- An **adjective** describes a noun. Examples: *dark* woods, *chilly* night

1. Decide whether each of these words is a noun, adjective, or verb. Write *n*, *a*, or *v* next to each word.

Bandersnatch _n_	gimble _v_	mome _n_	tulgey ____
borogove ____	Jabberwock ____	outgrabe ____	uffish ____
burbled ____	Jubjub ____	rath ____	vorpal ____
frabjous ____	manxome ____	slithy ____	wabe ____
galumphing ____	mimsy ____	toves ____	whiffling ____

2. Make up definitions for the following words. Follow the example.

Bandersnatch: _Noun. An animal that lives in the tulgey wood._
The Bandersnatch and Jubjub bird are mortal enemies.

Burble: _____

Frabjous: _____

Gimble: _____

Jabberwock: _____

Mimsy: _____

Slithy: _____

Tove: _____

Whiffle: _____

Wacky Words   **31**

Verse in Motion

Contents

Before You Read the Poem

Build Background

The following poem is like a snapshot. It describes a runner in mid-action, as if the scene were a single frame in a movie. With students, brainstorm a list of words that describe a professional runner in the middle of a sprint. Prompt students by asking them to describe the runner's muscles, the position of his arms and legs, and his immediate surroundings. Write their words and phrases on the board in the form of a word web.

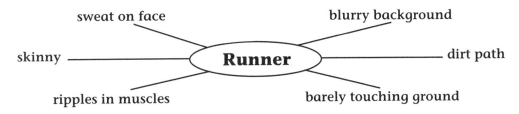

While You Read the Poem

The author of this poem, Walt Whitman, was very innovative in his use of spelling and punctuation. For example, he put an apostrophe in participles such as *well-train'd* and *rais'd*. The contracted form does not, however, change the pronunciation of these words. There are also many punctuation marks for a poem this short. Read the poem aloud, demonstrating how to pause at the commas. For the purpose of oral reading, the semicolons act as full stops. The long dash in the center of the poem signifies a pause slightly longer than the pause that accompanies a comma. The important thing is to pause in a natural way at the appropriate time to help make the imagery easy to visualize. After you have done a model reading, invite several volunteers to take turns reading the poem aloud.

After You Read the Poem

Elements of Poetry

Form: Free Verse This poem is written as free verse. There are no rhymes; neither is there a formal meter, although the first and last lines have fewer syllables than the pair of lines in the middle. Whitman used free verse to make the sound of his poems more familiar to ordinary people.

Poet's Toolbox: Descriptive Words "The Runner" uses many adjectives and other descriptive words. Using adjectives, as opposed to adverbs, helps to create the "snapshot" effect that the poet was seeking. Ask students to orally identify the adjectives in this poem. On the second activity page, they will list all the adjectives in the poem.

Follow-up Activities

Students may work independently to complete the activities on pages 35 and 36.

The Runner

On a flat road runs the well-train'd runner;
He is lean and sinewy, with muscular legs;
He is thinly clothed—he leans forward as he runs,
With lightly closed fists, and arms partially rais'd.

—*Walt Whitman*

 Did You Know? This poem comes from a book called *Leaves of Grass* by Walt Whitman. The book was reprinted about half a dozen times during the poet's life. Every time a new edition came out, Whitman changed the order of the poems, and he added new poems, too. Each edition was very different from the one before.

The Runner

Understanding the Poem

Read each question and choose the best answer. You may wish to reread "The Runner" as you work.

1. This poem describes what a runner looks like _____ .
   - (A) while he is running
   - (B) when he loses a race
   - (C) at the end of a marathon
   - (D) right before he is about to start a race

2. You can tell that the runner in this poem _____ .
   - (A) is out of shape
   - (B) has just started training
   - (C) runs on a regular basis
   - (D) doesn't care about winning

3. The opposite of *lean* is _____ .
   - (A) skinny
   - (B) overweight
   - (C) fully dressed
   - (D) barely dressed

4. The word *sinewy* probably has something to do with _____ .
   - (A) hair
   - (B) teeth
   - (C) bones
   - (D) muscles

5. The poet uses lots of details to _____ .
   - (A) paint a picture
   - (B) solve a puzzle
   - (C) create a feeling
   - (D) support an argument

Name _____

Understanding the Poem

This poem uses a lot of adjectives. An adjective helps to modify, or describe, a noun.

1. Write all the words and phrases that are used to describe the runner.

    _____

    _____

2. Write the phrases used to describe the runner's hands and arms.

    _____

3. Complete the following chart. In each column, write words and phrases that describe each of these athletes.

Jockey	Weight lifter	Ballerina	Boxer

4. Choose one of the athletes from the chart. Write a poem about that athlete using the words that you wrote. If you prefer, write about a different kind of athlete. Your poem doesn't have to rhyme. Use "The Runner" as a model if you need help.

    _____

    _____

    _____

    _____

Before You Read the Poem

Build Background

Tell students that this poem is told from the point of view of a young boy watching his father play basketball. In the poem, the boy compares his father to a force of nature. Ask students what kinds of comparisons they might expect to read about, based on the poem's title.

While You Read the Poem

Ask volunteers to take turns reading the poem aloud. There is no punctuation in the poem to show readers where to pause, but you may want to suggest that students pause at the end of the first line. The second and third lines can be read as one sentence.

After You Read the Poem

Elements of Poetry

Form: Haiku Write the poem on the board and have students help you determine the number of syllables in each line. Draw a slash after each syllable, showing students that the first and last lines have five syllables, and the second line has seven syllables. Tell students that this pattern is used in haiku, a poetic form that originated in Japan hundreds of years ago. Haiku is now used by many poets writing in English.

Poet's Toolbox: Alliteration and Consonance Alliteration is the repetition of consonant sounds at the beginning of words that are in close proximity to each other. The repetition of final consonant sounds is called *consonance*. In "Lightning Jumpshot," the poet has combined both of these techniques to create an interesting effect. In the first line, he contrasts /s/ and /z/ at the end of each word. In the next line, he achieves alliteration with the words *shoots* and *jumpshot*. Even though /sh/ is in the middle of *jumpshot*, it is at the beginning of the word *shot*, which is embedded in *jumpshot*, thereby achieving alliteration with *shoots*. In the last line, *sweaty storm* is also an alliterative pair, and *through* makes an alliterative pair with *thunder* in the first line. Throughout this poem, the poet contrasts the sounds of /s/, /z/, /sh/, and /j/, which are all related. They are formed in the front of the mouth with the teeth close together. Linguists call these sounds *fricatives* because they involve the vibration of the tongue. Have students pay attention to these contrasting sounds during oral readings of the poem.

Follow-up Activities

Students may work independently to complete the activities on pages 39 and 40.

Lightning Jumpshot

Daddy's voice thunders
he shoots a lightning jumpshot
through a sweaty storm

—*Michael Burgess*

Understanding the Poem

Read each question and choose the best answer. You may wish to reread "Lightning Jumpshot" as you work.

1. The narrator in this poem is _____.

    Ⓐ keeping score

    Ⓑ worried about the weather

    Ⓒ getting ready to join the game

    Ⓓ watching his father play basketball

2. The narrator compares his father to thunder and lightning to show how _____ he is.

    Ⓐ quick and forceful

    Ⓑ loud and scary

    Ⓒ hard to control

    Ⓓ dangerous

3. You can tell that the narrator's father is probably _____.

    Ⓐ tricky

    Ⓑ a good player

    Ⓒ outnumbered

    Ⓓ slow on his feet

4. The "sweaty storm" in the last line must be _____.

    Ⓐ dark clouds

    Ⓑ lightning and thunder

    Ⓒ the players on the other team

    Ⓓ the people watching the game

5. You can tell that the poem's narrator _____ his father.

    Ⓐ admires

    Ⓑ is afraid of

    Ⓒ wants to beat

    Ⓓ feels equal to

Name _____

Lightning Jumpshot

Understanding the Poem

In this poem, the poet contrasts the sounds of *s, sh,* and *z.* The same sound isn't always spelled with the same letter. For example, you hear the *z* sound at the end of the words *Daddy's* and *thunders.*

1. Read this list of words. Can you find the sounds of *s, sh,* and *z* in each word?

shake	knees	choose	skeleton
curse	scary	shampoo	sugar
see	shiver	pants	ice
freeze	legs	sidewalk	was
sure	face	skateboard	worse

2. Write the words above in the correct column. There should be five words in each column. Read the words aloud to check your work.

Words That Start with *s* Sound	Words That Start with *sh* Sound	Words That End with *s* Sound	Words That End with *z* Sound

3. Now, write sentences using words from each of the four lists. Use at least three words from the list in each sentence. The first one, using words that start with the *s* sound, has been done for you.

 <u>It would be scary to see a skeleton skateboard on a sidewalk.</u>

 _____

 _____

 _____

Read and Understand Poetry • EMC 3325 • ©2005 by Evan-Moor Corp.

Before You Read the Poem

Build Background

Tell students they are going to read a poem that compares walking and skating. To warm up, draw a Venn diagram with labels as shown. With students, brainstorm words that describe each activity and write them in the appropriate part of the diagram. Then write words that both activities have in common.

Review Mythological Reference

This poem includes a reference to Mercury, a figure from Greek mythology. Make sure students know that Mercury was a messenger to the gods on Mount Olympus. They may have seen images of him with small wings on his feet to help make him such a speedy messenger.

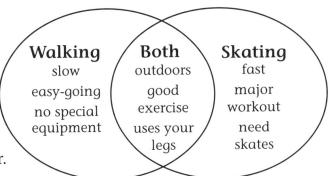

While You Read the Poem

Invite volunteers to take turns reading the poem aloud. Point out that students don't need to pause at the end of each line unless there is a comma or period.

After You Read the Poem

Elements of Poetry

Form: Free Verse Review with students the elements of free verse. There are no rhyming pairs and no formal rhythm patterns in free verse, but poets working with this form use other kinds of techniques that are particular to poetry. For example, poetry is much more tolerant of run-on sentences than is prose. In this poem, there are 12 lines but only three sentences. In addition, the poet also uses *personification*, another device that is commonly used in poetry. Next, present information to students on personification (below).

Poet's Toolbox: Personification Point out how in the first three lines of the poem, the narrator describes the trail as if it were able to grab her and make her struggle to walk uphill. When a poet describes a thing in human terms—whether the thing is natural or artificial—the poet is using a technique called *personification*. Students will further explore personification on the second activity page.

Follow-up Activities

Students may work independently to complete the activities on pages 43 and 44.

Skating the River Trail

When I walk the river trail
the ground grabs every step
and makes me pay for every hill,
but when I lace my skates and take
the same path, I am a magic runner
like Mercury, that statue at the museum
with wings on his heels.
I need only ease one foot past the other,
to feel fast air against my face.
Sometimes, on a curve,
        Or when someone is coming,
            I lean.

—*Linda Armstrong*

Understanding the Poem

Read each question and choose the best answer. You may wish to reread "Skating the River Trail" as you work.

1. This poem takes place _____ .
   - Ⓐ along a river
   - Ⓑ in a skating rink
   - Ⓒ on top of a mountain
   - Ⓓ in a suburban neighborhood

2. What is the poet saying when she writes that the trail "makes me pay for every hill"?
   - Ⓐ You can't skate for free.
   - Ⓑ It costs money to enter the trail.
   - Ⓒ She has to work hard to get up the hill.
   - Ⓓ She has to pray before she goes up each hill.

3. The narrator compares herself to Mercury because she _____ when she skates.
   - Ⓐ is so graceful
   - Ⓑ breaks all the rules
   - Ⓒ feels like she can fly
   - Ⓓ makes everybody look at her

4. What does it mean to "ease one foot past the other"?
   - Ⓐ Place the feet side by side.
   - Ⓑ Move feet back and forth as quickly.
   - Ⓒ Lift one foot so that it is slightly higher than the other.
   - Ⓓ Carefully but smoothly move each foot forward one at a time.

5. You can tell that the narrator is a _____ skater.
   - Ⓐ timid
   - Ⓑ strong
   - Ⓒ careful
   - Ⓓ hesitant

Understanding the Poem

Describing an animal, object, or idea as if it has human qualities is known as *personification*. Here are some examples:

The forest welcomed me with open arms.

Does a forest really have arms? That's just a figure of speech. It's a way of saying that you feel "at home" in the forest.

The long winding trail seemed to call my name.

Trails don't really talk. But when something looks tempting, we can say it "calls to us."

1. What are the two examples of personification in "Skating the River Trail"?

_____

2. Write in your own words what the poet means by this personification.

_____

_____

3. Complete the following table. Write some words to personify the object. Then explain why you chose that expression to personify that particular object. Look at the examples that are provided.

Object	Personifying Expression	Why It Makes Sense
forest	welcomed me with open arms	you can feel "at home" in a forest
trail	called my name	a trail can be tempting
skyscrapers	pointed at the sky	you look up at the sky to see skyscrapers
hands on clock		
blank page		
armchair		
cool breeze		
autumn leaves		

The Work of Our Hands

Contents

Before You Read the Poem

Build Background

Tell students that the poem they are going to read is about different kinds of workers. The poem was written in 1867. Ask students to brainstorm a list of jobs from the 1800s. Write their responses on the board in the form of a word web, as shown.

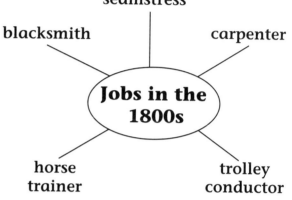

While You Read the Poem

Ask for eight volunteers to read the poem. Have one volunteer be the "narrator." He or she can read the first line and the last three lines. The other seven students may each read one of the remaining lines in the poem. When they are finished, have students switch roles, or form another group.

During one reading, review the occupations noted in the word web you created, checking off any that are mentioned in the poem. Did students guess many of the occupations that were featured in the poem?

After You Read the Poem

Elements of Poetry

Form: Free Verse This poem is written as free verse. There are no rhymes; neither is there a formal meter, or pattern of rhythm. Whitman used free verse to make the sound of his poems more familiar to ordinary people. Despite this, Whitman has always been seen as a literary giant, not "the voice of the masses" he sought to be.

Poet's Toolbox: Listing Listing, or *cataloging* as it is also called, is a technique that Whitman often used in his poetry. As the name suggests, listing is a way of naming a series of items in a certain category. In this poem, Whitman lists a range of occupations that were common in the 1800s. Some of these occupations may be unfamiliar to students. A hatter, for example, is a maker of hats. These days, that would be an unusual profession, but in the 1800s, it was very common. In fact, all of these occupations were part of the working class.

Follow-up Activities

Students may work independently to complete the activities on pages 48 and 49.

I Hear America Singing

1   I hear America singing, the varied carols I hear,

2   Those of mechanics, each one singing his as it should be
        blithe and strong;

3   The carpenter singing his as he measures his plank or beam,

4   The mason singing his as he makes ready for work,
        or leaves off work,

5   The boatman singing what belongs to him in his boat, the
        deckhand singing on the steamboat deck,

6   The shoemaker singing as he sits on his bench, the hatter
        singing as he stands,

7   The wood-cutter's song, the ploughboy's on his way in the
        morning, or at noon intermission or at sundown,

8   The delicious singing of the mother, or of the young wife
        at work, or of the girl sewing and washing,

9   Each singing what belongs to him or her and to none else,

10 The day what belongs to the day—at night the party of
        young fellows, robust, friendly,

11 Singing with open mouths their strong melodious songs.

—*Walt Whitman*

Understanding the Poem

Read each question and choose the best answer. You may wish to reread "I Hear America Singing" as you work.

1. This poem is about _____ .
   Ⓐ a parade of workers
   Ⓑ melodies and rhythms
   Ⓒ workers and their songs
   Ⓓ songs written for workers

2. Which of the following jobs is <u>not</u> mentioned in the poem?
   Ⓐ shoemaker
   Ⓑ blacksmith
   Ⓒ mechanic
   Ⓓ hatter

3. The carpenter is _____ the length of the wood.
   Ⓐ nailing
   Ⓑ sawing
   Ⓒ sanding
   Ⓓ calculating

4. The phrase "noon intermission" in line 7 means _____ .
   Ⓐ lunch break
   Ⓑ time to leave work
   Ⓒ a pause in the action
   Ⓓ the break in the middle of a play

5. The workers in this poem _____ .
   Ⓐ seem to like their jobs
   Ⓑ are tired and overworked
   Ⓒ look forward to the future
   Ⓓ sing to forget their problems

Read and Understand Poetry • EMC 3325 • ©2005 by Evan-Moor Corp.

Understanding the Poem

1. This poem is about workers and the songs they sing or sounds they make while they are working. List the different jobs mentioned in this poem.

   _____

   _____

   _____

2. If Walt Whitman had written "I Hear America Singing" today, what are seven jobs he might have included in this poem?

   _____

   _____

3. Using the jobs you have listed, rewrite "I Hear America Singing." Use the name of a different job for each blank line and say something about the kind of work that worker does.

   ### "I Hear America Singing"

   I hear America singing, the varied carols I hear,

   _____

   _____

   _____

   _____

   _____

   _____

   Each singing what belongs to him or her and to none else,

   The day what belongs to the day—at night the party of
      young fellows, robust, friendly,

   Singing with open mouths their strong melodious songs.

Before You Read the Poem

Build Background

Tell students that the poem they are going to read is about a blacksmith in a village, probably in New England in the early 1800s. Talk with students about blacksmithing, asking them to share what they know. In your discussion, include the following: Blacksmiths work with iron and other metals. They use a bellows to blow on coals, making the coals even hotter. Using tongs, a piece of iron is placed on top of the coals and heated. When it is glowing hot, the blacksmith puts the iron on an anvil and beats it into the shape he wants. These days, metalwork is usually done in a foundry or factory, although some blacksmiths still practice the craft. Back in the 1800s, blacksmithing was an honored trade. A blacksmith made many tools and instruments, such as horseshoes that were vital to village life. The village blacksmith took on an apprentice and taught the boy everything he knew, little by little. As cities grew larger and larger, people became nostalgic about the values and way of life that the blacksmith represented. Longfellow could sense this change coming on. His poem, "The Village Blacksmith," was written in 1836. In it, Longfellow pays homage to this time-honored craft, which was already slipping into memory. He portrays the blacksmith as a hardworking, honorable man.

While You Read the Poem

Ask for eight volunteers. Have each volunteer read one stanza of the poem. When the group is finished, other students may take turns reading as well.

After You Read the Poem

Elements of Poetry

Form: Rhyming Verse This poem is written in rhyming verse. Ask students to help you identify the rhyming pattern. In the first stanza, it is *ababcb*. In all other stanzas, it is *abcbdb*. Point out that rhyming words such as *door* and *roar* use different spelling patterns. Students will compare the spelling of these and other rhyming words on the second activity page.

Poet's Toolbox: Descriptive Words This poem is rich in adjectives and other descriptive words. Ask students to find adjectives that describe specific things in the poem, including the blacksmith's hands *(large, sinewy)*, arms *(brawny, strong as iron bands)*, hair *(crisp, black, and long)*, sledge *(heavy)*, and others.

Follow-up Activities

Students may work independently to complete the activities on pages 53 and 54.

The Village Blacksmith

1 Under a spreading chestnut-tree
       The village smithy stands;
   The smith, a mighty man is he,
       With large and sinewy hands;
   And the muscles of his brawny arms
       Are strong as iron bands.

2 His hair is crisp, and black, and long,
       His face is like the tan;
   His brow is wet with honest sweat,
       He earns whate'er he can,
   And looks the whole world in the face,
       For he owes not any man.

3 Week in, week out, from morn till night,
       You can hear his bellows blow;
   You can hear him swing his heavy sledge,
       With measured beat and slow,
   Like a sexton ringing the village bell,
       When the evening sun is low.

4 And children coming home from school
       Look in at the open door;
   They love to see the flaming forge,
       And hear the bellows roar,
   And catch the burning sparks that fly
       Like chaff from a threshing-floor.

5 He goes on Sunday to the church,
       And sits among his boys;
   He hears the parson pray and preach,
       He hears his daughter's voice,
   Singing in the village choir,
       And it makes his heart rejoice.

6 It sounds to him like her mother's voice,
    Singing in Paradise!
He needs must think of her once more,
    How in the grave she lies;
And with his hard, rough hand he wipes
    A tear out of his eyes.

7 Toiling,—rejoicing,—sorrowing,
    Onward through life he goes;
Each morning sees some task begin,
    Each evening sees it close;
Something attempted, something done,
    Has earned a night's repose.

8 Thanks, thanks to thee, my worthy friend,
    For the lesson thou hast taught!
Thus at the flaming forge of life
    Our fortunes must be wrought;
Thus on its sounding anvil shaped
    Each burning deed and thought.

                    —*Henry Wadsworth Longfellow*

Did You Know? Henry Wadsworth Longfellow was born in Portland, Maine, in 1807. He began his formal schooling at the age of three. When he was six, his teacher sent home this report about the young scholar: "Master Henry Longfellow is one of the best boys we have in school. He spells and reads very well. He can also add and multiply numbers. His conduct last quarter was very correct and amiable." By the age of 22, Longfellow had become a college professor of modern languages and literature, and had a long and productive career in both teaching and writing.

Name _____

Understanding the Poem

Read each question and choose the best answer. You may wish to reread "The Village Blacksmith" as you work.

1. This poem takes place in _____.
   - Ⓐ a Spanish mission
   - Ⓑ a Native American village
   - Ⓒ a small town a long time ago
   - Ⓓ an imaginary place that could never exist

2. The blacksmith _____.
   - Ⓐ works with his hands
   - Ⓑ keeps the village clean
   - Ⓒ is a pastor at the church
   - Ⓓ educates the town's children

3. Look at the seventh stanza. What might be another way to say "toiling, rejoicing, sorrowing"?
   - Ⓐ working with tools and instruments
   - Ⓑ getting the right tool for the right job
   - Ⓒ working through good times and bad times
   - Ⓓ working when you're happy, hiding when you're sad

4. You can tell that _____ are important values to the people in this village.
   - Ⓐ sharing and giving
   - Ⓑ honesty and hard work
   - Ⓒ cooperation and helpfulness
   - Ⓓ education and self-improvement

5. You can tell that the poet thinks the blacksmith _____.
   - Ⓐ should get back to basics
   - Ⓑ is a good model for the community
   - Ⓒ makes less money than he deserves
   - Ⓓ doesn't serve much purpose anymore

Name _____

The Village Blacksmith

Understanding the Poem

1. This poem is written in rhyming verse. A lot of the words that rhyme have totally different spellings. Look at these rhyming pairs:

tree	door	boys	lies	goes	taught
he	roar	voice	eyes	close	thought

   Now, read these pairs of words. Circle the words that rhyme. Cross out the words that don't rhyme.

rot/taught	choice/spice	voice/views	goes/does	floor/core
money/rely	sea/comedy	boys/noise	eyes/rise	drought/thought

2. Write a word that rhymes with each of these words. The words don't have to use the same spelling rules. Look at the words above for help.

   bought: _____

   chore: _____

   treaty: _____

   dice: _____

   crows: _____

   rejoice: _____

   cries: _____

   bumblebee: _____

   doze: _____

   toys: _____

3. Write a definition for these words as they are used in the poem. Use a dictionary if you need to.

   tan: _____

   bellows: _____

   chaff: _____

   repose: _____

Read and Understand Poetry • EMC 3325 • ©2005 by Evan-Moor Corp.

Before You Read the Poem

Build Background

Remind students that this poem is part of a unit called "The Work of Our Hands"; tell them that the next poem is about an artist. Lead a discussion with students about the artistic process. Start by saying that artists usually begin a project with raw material of some sort. A writer starts with a blank page, for example, and a sculptor starts with a lump of clay or a block of wood. Ask students: *What does a sculptor "see" when he or she looks at a lump of clay? Where do musicians and filmmakers get their ideas?* Invite students to share about an artistic project they have seen through completion. How did they start? What materials were necessary? What were some of the problems or obstacles along the way, and how were they overcome? Artists are often surprised by their creations. Invite student artists to share about the feelings they had upon completing a project.

While You Read the Poem

Invite volunteers to take turns reading the poem aloud for the class. Tell readers to pause at the commas, which sometimes appear in the middle of a line. You may suggest that readers slightly change their voices when reading the quotations of Don Luis. You may also explain that *Don* rhymes with *tone,* and is a title similar to "Mr." that precedes a given name. The *r* in *Mira* is pronounced with a slight roll; the word means "look." If you have native Spanish speakers in class, invite a volunteer to model the pronunciation of these words.

After You Read the Poem

Elements of Poetry

Form: Free Verse This poem is written as free verse, as it has no pattern of rhyme or meter. It almost reads like prose, and could be reformatted to look and read like several paragraphs of a personal narrative. It may have even started off that way. Poets sometimes reformat simple prose to look like stanzas in a poem. "What makes it poetry?" is a valid question. Ask for students' opinions. They might say that it zeroes in on a significant moment, or that Don Luis's artistic vision is a more suitable subject for a poem than a short story or essay. Share your own insights as well.

Poet's Toolbox: Alignment This poem is broken into two stanzas. The lines are all centered on the page, except for the last line in the first stanza. The "line" actually consists of a single word: *listening.* Ask students why they think the poet did this. When poets isolate a single word in this way, they draw attention to it. The poet may have wanted to show how important the act of listening is to the artist. By placing the word all the way to the end of the line like this, you can almost imagine Don Luis cocking his head to the side as he "listens" to the piece of wood.

Follow-up Activities

Students may work independently to complete the activities on pages 57 and 58.

Purple Snake

"It's in there, sleeping,"
Don Luis says and winks.
He knows I want to feel
the animal asleep in a piece of wood,
like he does
turning it this way and that
listening.

Slowly he strokes the wood,
rough and wrinkled. Like his hands.
He begins to carve his way.
"*Mira*. Its head, its scales, its tail."
Don Luis rubs and strokes
the animal before he paints
its eyes open.
When the paint dries,
I place the purple snake
by the green bull and red frog
that Don Luis found asleep
in a piece of wood.

—*Pat Mora*

Name _____

Purple Snake

Understanding the Poem

Read each question and choose the best answer. You may wish to reread "Purple Snake" as you work.

1. Don Luis is _____.
   - Ⓐ a poet
   - Ⓑ a singer
   - Ⓒ a painter
   - Ⓓ a sculptor

2. Look at the first stanza. Why does Don Luis say that the snake is "asleep"?
   - Ⓐ He can't hear it.
   - Ⓑ He won't look at it.
   - Ⓒ Its eyes are closed.
   - Ⓓ It hasn't been carved yet.

3. Look at the second stanza. The word *strokes* means _____.
   - Ⓐ taps lightly
   - Ⓑ gently touches
   - Ⓒ whittles with a knife
   - Ⓓ rubs the palms of his hands together

4. You can tell from this poem that Don Luis has also carved _____.
   - Ⓐ two sleeping animals
   - Ⓑ a rough and wrinkled frog
   - Ⓒ a green bull and a red frog
   - Ⓓ a purple snake with green scales

5. Don Luis uses _____ colors to paint his carvings.
   - Ⓐ fanciful
   - Ⓑ realistic
   - Ⓒ plain
   - Ⓓ pale

Understanding the Poem

1. *Prose* is ordinary written language such as sentences and paragraphs. In a way, this poem is like prose. The poet broke the lines to make it look like a poem, but the two stanzas are just like two paragraphs from a story.

Write a paragraph that you could turn into a poem. Describe something interesting or funny that you saw. Or tell about a conversation you had with somebody you know. It should be about a special moment that made you think "Aha!" Include dialog and as many descriptive words as you can.

_____

_____

_____

_____

_____

_____

2. Now, break the paragraph into lines so that it looks like poetry. When you are finished, share your work with a classmate.

_____

_____

_____

_____

_____

_____

_____

_____

_____

_____

_____

Before You Read the Poem

Build Background

The following poem is a dialog between a mother and her daughter. The young girl is wondering about her future, and her mother is encouraging her to dream big dreams. No matter what she winds up doing, the girl decides that she wants to be just like her mother. Invite students to share about an adult that they admire. It may be a parent, caregiver, aunt, uncle, friend, teacher, or another special person in their life. Ask: *What do you admire about this person?* Tell students they will be reading a poem about a girl who admires her mother because she is caring and wise.

Introduce Vocabulary in Spanish

This poem uses a few words and phrases in Spanish. *M'ija,* for example, is a contraction of the two words *Mi* and *hija,* and is a loving expression meaning "my little daughter." The *j* is pronounced like an *h:* MEE-ha. *Arroz con pollo* is a traditional Mexican dish of rice and chicken. The *rr* in *arroz* is pronounced with a roll, and the *ll* in *pollo* is pronounced like *y:* POH-yoh. *Gozo* means "enjoyment," and is pronounced GOH-soh. *Mami* is a way to say *mother,* and is pronounced MAH-mee. Invite any Spanish speakers in the class to model pronunciation of these words.

While You Read the Poem

Ask two volunteers to read the poem aloud for the class. One student can take the role of the mother. Her lines are printed in italics. The other student can take the role of the little girl. When they are finished, invite another pair of students to read the poem aloud for the class.

After You Read the Poem

Elements of Poetry

Form: Stanzas This poem is written as free verse. There is no meter or rhyming pattern, but it is organized into stanzas. A stanza is equivalent to a paragraph in prose. It is a group of related sentences. Here, the poet has grouped together the words of each speaker into separate stanzas. This helps the reader keep track of who is speaking.

Poet's Toolbox: Dialog This poem is written entirely as a dialog. There is no commentary or narration by the poet. This way of writing poetry helps to create an atmosphere of familiarity and intimacy. It also helps to create characters that the reader can easily identify. Encourage students to share other ideas about why poets may choose to write poetry in dialog.

Follow-up Activities

Students may work independently to complete the activities on pages 61 and 62.

Growing Up

When I grow up,
I want to be a doctor.

M'ija, you will patch scraped knees
and wipe away children's tears.

But what if I become an architect?

M'ija, you will build beautiful houses
where children will sing and play.

And what if I become a teacher?

M'ija, you will teach
your students to read every day.

But what if I become a famous chef?

M'ija, your arroz con pollo
will be eaten with gozo.

And Mami, what if I want to be like you someday?

M'ija, why do you want to be like me?

Oh Mami, because you care for people, our house is built on love,
you are wise, and your spicy stew tastes delicious.

—*Liz Ann Báez Aguilar*

Understanding the Poem

Read each question and choose the best answer. You may wish to reread "Growing Up" as you work.

1. This poem is written in the form of _____.
   - Ⓐ a list
   - Ⓑ a dialog
   - Ⓒ a description
   - Ⓓ a theatrical production

2. The two speakers are _____.
   - Ⓐ impossible to identify
   - Ⓑ a teacher and student
   - Ⓒ a mother and daughter
   - Ⓓ really just one person speaking to herself

3. An *architect* must be somebody who _____.
   - Ⓐ makes food
   - Ⓑ builds houses
   - Ⓒ takes care of children
   - Ⓓ teaches at private schools

4. The mother wants her daughter to _____.
   - Ⓐ be just like her
   - Ⓑ behave herself
   - Ⓒ do whatever she wants
   - Ⓓ become a teacher, not a chef

5. The girl thinks that her mother _____.
   - Ⓐ is just like a friend
   - Ⓑ is caring, loving, and wise
   - Ⓒ might become a famous chef
   - Ⓓ works too hard most of the time

Name _____

Growing Up

Understanding the Poem

This poem is written in the form of a dialog between a girl and her mother. What if the conversation were between a boy and his father? How would the conversation be different? Show your ideas by completing the dialog below.

Boy: _____ Dad, when I grow up, I want to work outside._____

_____ I like working with my hands._____

Father: _____ I like working outside, too. What kinds of jobs do you_____

_____ like the most?_____

Boy: _____

_____

Father: _____

_____

Boy: _____

_____

Father: _____

_____

Boy: _____

_____

Father: _____

_____

Boy: _____

_____

Father: _____

_____

62 *The Work of Our Hands*   Read and Understand Poetry • EMC 3325 • ©2005 by Evan-Moor Corp.

On the Railroad

Contents

Before You Read the Poems

Build Background

The following poems are by Carl Sandburg, a poet who is often compared to Walt Whitman. Ask students what they remember about the two poems they have read by Walt Whitman: "The Runner" and "I Hear America Singing." Tell students that, like Whitman, Sandburg wrote mostly in free verse. His poems describe American people, cities, and landscapes. Among his first volumes of poetry is a book called *Chicago Poems*. It was written in 1916. At the time, Chicago was a rising industrial city. In fact, it was called "America's Second City," being second only to New York. Sandburg thought the smokestacks, railroads, and bustling city streets were beautiful to look at, and he wanted to evoke that beauty in his poetry. The poems students wil read next are from *Chicago Poems*.

While You Read the Poems

Invite volunteers to read each poem aloud. Tell the reader that the poems are set during a train trip late at night. Encourage the reader to use a soft tone of voice suited to the atmosphere of the poems.

After You Read the Poems

Elements of Poetry

Form: Free Verse "Window" almost feels like haiku in its brevity and simplicity. The syllable pattern is also similar to haiku in a general way because the first and last lines have more syllables than the middle line, but the exact syllable count does not match the haiku pattern. Both of these poems are better characterized as free verse, since they do not follow any established rules or formulae. Point out to students that many poets like to work with free verse because of the freedom it gives them to create an original, unique poem that is unlike any other.

Poet's Toolbox: Imagery These poems are made up of words and phrases that describe a train ride late at night. They do a great job of creating atmosphere by evoking the senses of sight and sound. Ask students what other words or phrases the poet might have used to describe these late-night scenes.

Follow-up Activities

Students may work independently to complete the activities on pages 66 and 67.

Night Train

Window

Night from a railroad car window
Is a great, dark, soft thing
Broken across with slashes of light.

Home

Here is a thing my heart wishes the world had more of:
I heard it in the air of one night when I listened
To a mother singing softly to a child restless and angry
in the darkness.

from "Poems Done on a Late Night Car"
—Carl Sandburg

Did You Know? Carl Sandburg was born to Swedish immigrant parents in Galesburg, Illinois, in 1878. His father worked as a blacksmith's helper for the railroad. Carl left school after eighth grade and worked for ten years before traveling for a year as a hobo. Sandburg eventually finished college and worked as a journalist. He published his first book of poetry in 1924, and later wrote books for children as well. He also became famous for his biography of Abraham Lincoln.

Night Train

Understanding the Poems

Read each question and choose the best answer. You may wish to reread the Night Train poems as you work.

1. These poems tell about the poet's thoughts and feelings _____.
   - Ⓐ about growing old
   - Ⓑ during a train trip
   - Ⓒ from his childhood
   - Ⓓ while looking out his window at home

2. Both of these poems take place _____.
   - Ⓐ late at night
   - Ⓑ in broad daylight
   - Ⓒ at the crack of dawn
   - Ⓓ at the same exact time

3. In the first poem, the poet compares the night to _____.
   - Ⓐ a window
   - Ⓑ a ray of light
   - Ⓒ a railroad car
   - Ⓓ a great, dark, soft thing

4. In the second poem, you can tell that the poet thinks _____.
   - Ⓐ it's a small world
   - Ⓑ the world is perfect just the way it is
   - Ⓒ there are too many children in the world
   - Ⓓ the world would be better if more people acted kindly

5. In both of these poems, it sounds like the poet is probably _____.
   - Ⓐ at home
   - Ⓑ going to work
   - Ⓒ traveling alone
   - Ⓓ spending time with his family

   Read and Understand Poetry • EMC 3325 • ©2005 by Evan-Moor Corp.

Name _____

Night Train

Understanding the Poems

Imagine that you are on a train late at night. Take a moment to imagine what you might see, hear, smell, and feel. Then answer these questions.

1. Where have you been?

_____

2. Where are you going?

_____

3. What kinds of things do you see out the window?

_____

4. What do you see around you on the train?

_____

5. What do you hear?

_____

6. What kinds of smells are around you?

_____

7. How does your body feel? What do you feel with your skin?

_____

8. What are you thinking about?

_____

9. If you like, you might want to use your answers to write a short poem. You may share the poem with a classmate or friend. Use another sheet of paper.

©2005 by Evan-Moor Corp. • EMC 3325 • Read and Understand Poetry **On the Railroad** 67

Before You Read the Poem

Build Background

The following poem is by Henry David Thoreau, a philosopher and writer from the nineteenth century. You might share some of the following information with students before you read the poem: Thoreau graduated from Harvard University, one of the country's top-rated schools. After that, he was a teacher for a while. In his classes, he taught students about the importance of living a simple life. To help make his point, he lived in a small hut by a pond for two years from 1845 to 1847. The book he wrote about those two years is called *Walden*, and it is still required reading in many high schools and universities. Introduce the poem, telling students that it tells about the growth of the railroads, which were very new in Thoreau's time. Ask students to predict what a nature-lover like Thoreau might think about the railroad.

While You Read the Poem

Invite a volunteer to read the poem aloud, pointing out that he or she should pause at the commas and periods. The second and third lines should be read with a barely perceptible pause between them. The two lines make a simple sentence without a break, but there needs to be a slight pause on *see* to bring out the rhyme with *me* at the end of the first line.

After You Read the Poem

Elements of Poetry

Form: Rhyming Verse This poem is made up of three rhyming couplets. The third line is on its own—it does not end with a rhyme. Having one "odd line" that doesn't rhyme with the others helps to make the poem a little more balanced. Without it, the poem would sound a little too simplistic and singsong. You can try reading the poem aloud without the third line to demonstrate this point. Then read the whole poem aloud again and ask students to identify the rhyming pattern, which is *aabccdd*.

Poet's Toolbox: Colloquial Language Point out that the expressions *a-blowing* and *a-growing* were common in the nineteenth century, although they are hardly ever used now. They simply mean *blowing* and *growing*. The hyphenated *a-* was a form of colloquial language that was often used whenever an extra syllable was needed to get the right meter. Colloquial language such as this makes the narrator sound like "country folk," which was an intended effect in this poem because a contrast is being set up between the distant city and the simple ways of the country.

Follow-up Activities

Students may work independently to complete the activities on pages 70 and 71.

What's the Railroad to Me?

What's the railroad to me?
I never go to see
Where it ends.

It fills a few hollows,
And makes banks for the swallows,
It sets the sand a-blowing,
And the blackberries a-growing.

—Henry David Thoreau

 Did You Know? Henry David Thoreau thought that people should return to nature. He left the city and lived in a simple hut by a pond, making all his own clothes and food. This was back in the 1800s, before there were even electric light bulbs. What would he think about technology today?

Understanding the Poem

Read each question and choose the best answer. You may wish to reread "What's the Railroad to Me?" as you work.

1. In this poem, the poet is watching the train pass through _____.
   - Ⓐ ghost towns
   - Ⓑ a train depot
   - Ⓒ a bustling city
   - Ⓓ the countryside

2. When the poet says he never goes to see where the railroad "ends," he means the _____.
   - Ⓐ city
   - Ⓑ end of time
   - Ⓒ wild, wild West
   - Ⓓ edge of the world

3. A *hollow* must be _____.
   - Ⓐ a nest
   - Ⓑ farmland
   - Ⓒ a small valley
   - Ⓓ the top of a hill

4. In this poem, *bank* means _____.
   - Ⓐ a bench or table
   - Ⓑ a mound of earth
   - Ⓒ the shore of a river
   - Ⓓ a place to keep money

5. The poet is saying that the railroad is _____.
   - Ⓐ a sign of the times
   - Ⓑ necessary for progress
   - Ⓒ just part of the landscape
   - Ⓓ something evil we must live with

Understanding the Poem

Henry David Thoreau wrote this poem in the 1800s, when steam trains were new. This new technology changed the United States drastically. Since then, there have been many new inventions. Think about how inventions bring change, and answer the following questions:

1. What did the railroad "mean" to Henry David Thoreau?

_____

_____

_____

2. What does the railroad "mean" to you? Think about how it affects your life, whether you use it or not.

_____

_____

_____

3. What changes did railroads and trains bring to the United States in the 1800s?

_____

_____

_____

4. The Internet is a new and growing technology, just like trains were in the 1800s. What kind of changes has the Internet brought? In what ways are these two forms of technology similar?

_____

_____

_____

5. What does the Internet "mean" to you?

_____

_____

_____

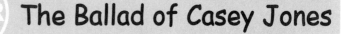

Before You Read the Poem

Build Background

The railway system grew swiftly in the second half of the nineteenth century. When the Transcontinental Railroad was completed in 1869, Americans could finally travel from the East Coast to San Francisco. This rapidly developing form of transportation stimulated people's imagination. Songs, stories, and sayings circulated about the men who built and operated the mighty "Iron Horse." This poem is an example. "The Ballad of Casey Jones" is a fairly accurate record of a real event. It was written by Wallace Saunders, an engine wiper and close friend of Casey Jones. Jones was an engineer who was well known for his distinctive whistle.

On April 30, 1900, Casey Jones agreed to take on an extra shift for another engineer. At about four o'clock in the morning, he was approaching the town of Vaughn, Mississippi. As he came around a bend, he saw a train stopped on the main line. It was too long to fit completely onto the sidetrack where the engineer had brought it to a halt. At 50 miles an hour (not 70, as the poem says), Casey couldn't stop his train in time. His Cannonball Special crashed and derailed. The fireman, Sim Webb, jumped out right before the crash. Miraculously, he was uninjured, but Casey "died at the throttle, with the whistle in his hand."

While You Read the Poem

Shortly after Jones's death, Wallace Saunders wrote this dramatic tale in verse and began to sing it to an original tune. Later, the verses were set to new music and eventually became a vaudeville attraction. If you can find a recording, teach your class how to sing the song. Or, invite volunteers to take turns reading each stanza aloud.

After You Read the Poem

Elements of Poetry

Form: Ballad This poem is a ballad, a long poem that tells a story, usually as a song. As with most ballads, it is written in quatrains, or stanzas made up of four lines each. The predominant rhyming pattern is *aabb*, although there are several stanzas that rhyme in the pattern *abab*. The stanzas with this alternate rhyming pattern serve as a refrain, or chorus, as described below.

Poet's Toolbox: Refrain Direct students' attention to the second, fifth, tenth, and last stanzas; they have the *abab* rhyming pattern. Ask students how these stanzas differ from the other stanzas in the poem. Students may notice that the *abab* rhyming pattern is different from the rest of the stanzas, which follow an *aabb* pattern. The meter of these stanzas is also shorter than the meter established by the first stanza, and each line within them is very similar in structure. With their simplicity, brevity, and repetition, they serve as a refrain, or chorus.

Follow-up Activities

Students may work independently to complete the activities on pages 75 and 76.

The Ballad of Casey Jones

1 Come all you rounders if you want to hear
   A story 'bout a brave engineer,
   Casey Jones was the rounder's name
   'Twas on the Illinois Central that he won his fame.

2 Casey Jones, he loved a locomotive.
   Casey Jones, a mighty man was he.
   Casey Jones run his final locomotive
   With the Cannonball Special on the old I.C.

3 Casey pulled into Memphis on Number Four,
   The engine foreman met him at the roundhouse door;
   Said, "Joe Lewis won't be able to make his run
   So you'll have to double out on Number One."

4 "If I can have Sim Webb, my fireman, my engine 382,
   Although I'm tired and weary, I'll take her through.
   Put on my whistle that come in today
   'Cause I mean to keep her wailing as we ride and pray."

5 Casey Jones mounted the cabin,
   Casey Jones, with the orders in his hand.
   Casey Jones, he mounted the cabin,
   Started on his farewell journey to the promised land.

6 They pulled out of Memphis nearly two hours late,
   Soon they were speeding at a terrible rate.
   And the people knew by the whistle's moan
   That the man at the throttle was Casey Jones.

7 "Need more coal there, fireman Sim,
   Open that door and heave it in.
   Give that shovel all you got
   And we'll reach Canton on the dot."

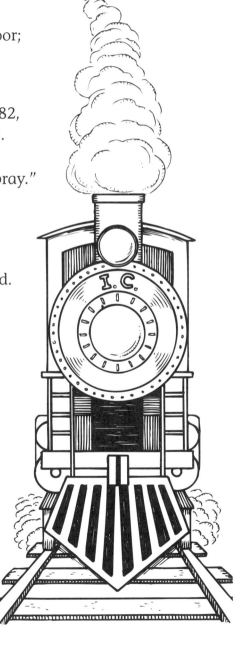

8 On April 30, 1900, that rainy morn,
   Down in Mississippi near the town of Vaughn,
   Sped the Cannonball Special only two minutes late,
   Traveling 70 miles an hour when they saw a freight.

9 The caboose number 83 was on the main line,
   Casey's last words were, "Jump, Sim, while you have the time."
   At 3:52 that morning came the fateful end,
   Casey took his farewell trip to the promised land.

10 Casey Jones, he died at the throttle,
   With the whistle in his hand.
   Casey Jones, he died at the throttle,
   But we'll all see Casey in the promised land.

11 His wife and three children were left to mourn
   The tragic death of Casey on that April morn.
   May God through His goodness keep them by His grace
   'Till they all meet together in that heavenly place.

12 Casey's body lies buried in Jackson, Tennessee
   Close beside the tracks of the old I.C.
   May his spirit live forever throughout the land
   As the greatest of all heroes of a railroad man.

13 Casey Jones, he died at the throttle,
   Casey Jones, with the whistle in his hand.
   Casey Jones, he died at the throttle,
   But we'll all see Casey in the promised land.

—*Wallace Saunders*

Read and Understand Poetry • EMC 3325 • ©2005 by Evan-Moor Corp.

Understanding the Poem

Read each question and choose the best answer. You may wish to reread
"The Ballad of Casey Jones" as you work.

1. The Illinois Central, or I.C., was the name of _____.
   - Ⓐ a train
   - Ⓑ a hotel
   - Ⓒ a train station
   - Ⓓ a railroad line

2. On the day of the accident, we know that Casey _____.
   - Ⓐ was tired
   - Ⓑ wasn't paying attention
   - Ⓒ wasn't really able to operate the train
   - Ⓓ was busy talking to Sim Webb, the fireman

3. Casey's train crashed by _____.
   - Ⓐ jumping off the rails
   - Ⓑ running through a red light
   - Ⓒ hitting another train head-on
   - Ⓓ ramming into a caboose on the main line

4. When the poem says that Casey "took his farewell trip to the promised land,"
   it means he _____.
   - Ⓐ got carried to the hospital
   - Ⓑ died and went to heaven
   - Ⓒ said good-bye to everybody
   - Ⓓ hung up his hat and went home

5. After the train crash, _____.
   - Ⓐ people still admired Casey
   - Ⓑ Casey was nowhere to be found
   - Ⓒ Casey's wife and children were ashamed
   - Ⓓ thousands of people came to Casey's funeral

Name _____

The Ballad of Casey Jones

Understanding the Poem

1. This poem is like a story. What is the sequence of events in the story? Read the following sentences. Write *1* next to the first event, *2* next to the second event, and so on.

_____ Another train is on the main line.

_____ Casey agrees, as long as he can use his own engine and take Sim Webb with him.

_____ The great engineer, Casey Jones, is buried in Jackson, Tennessee.

_____ The Cannonball nears Vaughn at about 4 o'clock in the morning.

_____ Casey tells Webb to jump out of the Cannonball, and he does.

_____ The Cannonball crashes, and Casey Jones is killed.

_____ The engine foreman tells Casey that he has to take over for Joe Lewis.

_____ The Number Four train arrives in Memphis.

_____ To make up for lost time, Casey made the Cannonball Special go at full speed.

2. Now, write the story of Casey Jones in the space below. Put all the verbs in the past tense. Make any changes you need to make so that the story flows smoothly. Share your work with a partner.

_____

_____

_____

_____

_____

_____

_____

_____

_____

_____

Read and Understand Poetry • EMC 3325 • ©2005 by Evan-Moor Corp.

Water and Waves

Contents

Before You Read the Poem

Build Background

This poem was written by Alfred, Lord Tennyson, one of the great poets of the English language. In 1850, Tennyson was named poet laureate of England. The tradition of bestowing this title upon a poet of the highest distinction began in England in 1616. The poet laureate seeks to raise an appreciation of poetry throughout the country.

Build Vocabulary

This poem uses some archaic vocabulary. Teach students the meaning of the following:

coot and hern: aquatic birds

cresses: leafy plants that grow near water

fallow: land that is unseeded

foreland: a projecting landmass

grayling: a small fry, or fish

haunt: a favorite place

mallow: a pink flower

sally: a leap forward

thorpe: a hamlet

Students need not memorize these words, as they are not very useful to know, but they are fun to say and are used by the poet, at least in part, for that very reason.

While You Read the Poem

Ask different students to read different sections of the poem. If there are at least thirteen students in your class, they can take turns reading individual stanzas. If not, assign two or three stanzas to each student. Help with pronunciation as needed.

After You Read the Poem

Elements of Poetry

Form: Rhyming Verse Help students identify the rhyming pattern in this poem, which is *abab*. Point out that the rhyming pair in the refrain, *river* and *ever*, is a "soft rhyme" because the vowel sound in the last syllable of each word is "closed" by the final *r*. With r-controlled vowels such as these, the rhyme can be strengthened by matching the vowel sound in the next-to-last syllable. A stronger rhyming pair, for example, would have been *river* and *shiver*, or *never* and *ever*. The poet probably concluded that the "soft" rhyming pair *river* and *ever* was strengthened by its repetition throughout the poem.

Poet's Toolbox: Alliteration Alliteration is the appearance of two words in close proximity that start with the same consonant sound. An example is "sudden sally," which appears in the second line of the poem. Ask students to find other examples of alliteration in the poem. Make sure that they include "field and fallow," "men may come," "fairy foreland," "foamy flake," "golden gravel," and "skimming swallows." In addition, students may notice that certain lines such as "I murmur under moon and stars" also contain alliteration, even though the two words starting with the same letter don't appear side by side.

Follow-up Activities

Students may work independently to complete the activities on pages 81 and 82.

The Brook

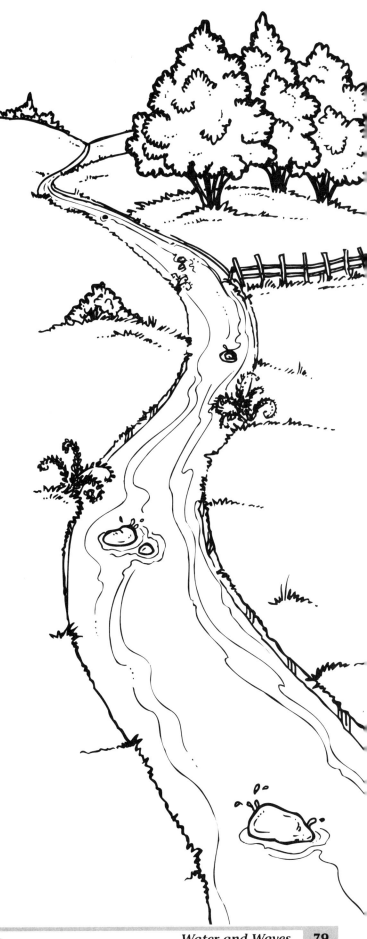

1 I come from haunts of coot and hern,
   I make a sudden sally
And sparkle out among the fern,
   To bicker down a valley.

2   By thirty hills I hurry down,
    Or slip between the ridges,
  By twenty thorpes, a little town,
    And half a hundred bridges.

3   Till last by Philip's farm I flow
    To join the brimming river,
For men may come and men may go,
    But I go on for ever.

4   I chatter over stony ways,
    In little sharps and trebles,
   I bubble into eddying bays,
    I babble on the pebbles.

5 With many a curve my banks I fret
   By many a field and fallow,
And many a fairy foreland set
With willow-weed and mallow.

6   I chatter, chatter, as I flow
    To join the brimming river,
For men may come and men may go,
    But I go on for ever.

7   I wind about, and in and out,
With here a blossom sailing,
And here and there a lusty trout,
And here and there a grayling,

8   And here and there a foamy flake
Upon me, as I travel
With many a silvery waterbreak
Above the golden gravel,

9   And draw them all along, and flow
To join the brimming river
For men may come and men may go,
But I go on for ever.

10   I steal by lawns and grassy plots,
I slide by hazel covers;
I move the sweet forget-me-nots
That grow for happy lovers.

11   I slip, I slide, I gloom, I glance,
Among my skimming swallows;
I make the netted sunbeam dance
Against my sandy shallows.

12   I murmur under moon and stars
In brambly wildernesses;
I linger by my shingly bars;
I loiter round my cresses;

13   And out again I curve and flow
To join the brimming river,
For men may come and men may go,
But I go on for ever.

—Alfred, Lord Tennyson

Read and Understand Poetry • EMC 3325 • ©2005 by Evan-Moor Corp.

Name _____

Understanding the Poem

Read each question and choose the best answer. You may wish to reread "The Brook" as you work.

1. This poem describes the path of a brook _____.
   - Ⓐ up a mountain
   - Ⓑ until it joins a river
   - Ⓒ on its way over a waterfall
   - Ⓓ until it completely disappears

2. One of the last places that the brook passes is _____.
   - Ⓐ a lawn
   - Ⓑ a farmhouse
   - Ⓒ a stone bridge
   - Ⓓ a field of flowers

3. When the poet says that the brook "babbles," he's referring to the _____.
   - Ⓐ twists and turns it takes
   - Ⓑ bubbles that rise to its surface
   - Ⓒ way it shines and sparkles in the sun
   - Ⓓ sound it makes as it washes over rocks and stones

4. Look at stanza 12. The poet uses the words *linger* and *loiter* to show how the brook _____.
   - Ⓐ never stops moving
   - Ⓑ can't make up its mind
   - Ⓒ slows down in some places
   - Ⓓ swirls around in circles

5. The poet seems to be saying that nature _____.
   - Ⓐ is more powerful than any machine
   - Ⓑ will go on no matter what people do
   - Ⓒ cannot keep up with the growth of cities
   - Ⓓ can teach us many things if only we would listen

The Brook

Understanding the Poem

1. This poem tells about the way a brook sounds and moves as it makes its way to the river. Complete the following chart. Use words from the poem to show how water sounds and how it moves. Add words of your own, too. Then do the same for "Fire" and "Wind."

Water		Fire		Wind	
Sounds	Movement	Sounds	Movement	Sounds	Movement

2. Using words from the chart, write your own sentence about water. The sentence can be about a waterfall, the ocean, or water coming out of a faucet.

_____

3. Now, write a sentence about a fire. You might write about a cozy fire at home or a raging forest fire.

_____

4. Finally, write a poem about wind. It might be a soft, gentle breeze or a fierce tornado.

_____

_____

_____

_____

Read and Understand Poetry • EMC 3325 • ©2005 by Evan-Moor Corp.

Before You Read the Poem

Build Background

Tell students that they are going to read a poem that is based on a sea shanty. Explain that sea shanties were sung by sailors while they raised the sails on a ship. It could take hours to raise these massive sails; singing prevented sailors from getting too bored, and it also helped to synchronize their movements. Sometimes sailors stomped their feet in time to the music, and on special occasions there might have been a drum or flute to accompany them. The songs were about life at sea. They reflected the sailors' hopes, worries, and superstitions. One superstition concerned mermaids. According to oldtimers, the sight of a mermaid was a bad omen; it might even signal a looming shipwreck. The following poem is taken from a sea shanty about the seafaring myth of the mermaid.

Build Vocabulary

In the last two lines of the chorus, reference is made to "landlubbers...below." Students will probably know that a landlubber is a person who never ventures out to sea, but they may not understand what is meant by *below*. It refers to people who live in the lowlands far from the sea.

While You Read the Poem

This poem was written to be sung. If you can't find the melody with an online search, you may wish to invite your students to create an original melody. To read the verses rather than sing them, one student can read the lyrics aloud, and the class can read the chorus in unison.

After You Read the Poem

Elements of Poetry

Form: Ballad Sea shanties like this one were often sung as ballads, which is a long singing poem that tells a story. This one is at least three hundred years old. As with most ballads, it is written in quatrains, or stanzas made up of four lines each. The predominant rhyming pattern is *abcb*, except for the chorus, which follows the pattern *abcbb*. The chorus is not a quatrain because it has five lines, but the fifth line is basically an "echo" of the fourth line.

Poet's Toolbox: Chorus Explain to students that the chorus of a song appears at regular intervals throughout a song. It is usually sung and worded the same way each time. In most cases, one person sings the lyrics, and a group of people sing the chorus. Ask students to provide examples of a chorus from songs that they know.

Follow-up Activities

Students may work independently to complete the activities on pages 85 and 86.

The Mermaid

'Twas Friday morn when we set sail,
And we had not got far from land,
When the Captain, he spied a lovely mermaid,
With a comb and a glass in her hand.

Chorus
Oh the ocean waves may roll,
And the stormy winds may blow,
While we poor sailors go skipping aloft
And the landlubbers lay down below, below, below
And the landlubbers lay down below.

Then up spoke the Captain of our gallant ship,
And a jolly old Captain was he;
"I have a wife in Salem town,
But tonight a widow she will be."

Chorus

Then up spoke the Cook of our gallant ship,
And a greasy old Cook was he;
"I care more for my kettles and my pots,
Than I do for the roaring of the sea."

Chorus

Then up spoke the Cabin-boy of our gallant ship,
And a dirty little brat was he;
"I have friends in Boston town
That don't care a ha' penny for me."

Chorus

Then three times 'round went our gallant ship,
And three times 'round went she,
And the third time that she went 'round
She sank to the bottom of the sea.

—Traditional

Did You Know? Back in the "Age of Sail" (the fifteenth to the eighteenth centuries), it was bad luck to see a mermaid. Sailors believed it was a sign that the ship was going to sink.

Read and Understand Poetry • EMC 3325 • ©2005 by Evan-Moor Corp.

The Mermaid

Understanding the Poem

Read each question and choose the best answer. You may wish to reread "The Mermaid" as you work.

1. The ship and its crew sank _____.
   - Ⓐ three times
   - Ⓑ for no reason at all
   - Ⓒ because it smashed into a rock
   - Ⓓ after coming across a mermaid

2. The glass in the mermaid's hand must have been _____.
   - Ⓐ a mirror
   - Ⓑ a telescope
   - Ⓒ a crystal ball
   - Ⓓ a drinking glass

3. Why did the Captain say that his wife was going to be a widow?
   - Ⓐ He knew he was going to die.
   - Ⓑ She was waiting for him at home.
   - Ⓒ They lived together at a lighthouse.
   - Ⓓ It was too late for her to get on the ship.

4. Which of the following characters is <u>not</u> mentioned in the poem?
   - Ⓐ the cook
   - Ⓑ the pilot
   - Ⓒ the captain
   - Ⓓ the cabin-boy

5. The quotes in the song give the crew's _____.
   - Ⓐ name and profession
   - Ⓑ most prized possessions
   - Ⓒ final words before they die
   - Ⓓ best wishes to everybody back home

Understanding the Poem

1. Before the ship sank, each member of the crew had something to say. What were they thinking when they said these things? Imagine how they must have felt, and then write a sentence describing their feelings.

What the Captain said:

"I have a wife in Salem town, but tonight a widow she will be."

What the Captain felt: _____

_____

_____

What the Cook said:

"I care more for my kettles and my pots, than I do for the roaring of the sea."

What the Cook felt: _____

_____

_____

What the Cabin-boy said:

"I have friends in Boston town that don't care a ha' penny for me."

What the Cabin-boy felt: _____

_____

_____

2. Sailors believed that their ship would sink if they saw a mermaid. Beliefs like this are called *superstitions*. A superstition is a belief that usually has to do with good luck or bad luck. Superstitions can't be proven because they aren't based on reason. Write about superstitions that you have heard of.

_____

_____

_____

_____

_____

Before You Read the Poem

Build Background

Tell students that the poem they are about to read is from *The Tempest,* a play by William Shakespeare. In the play's first act, Prospero the magician causes a ship to crash on a deserted isle. The crew and passengers are scattered about the island, not knowing who has survived. As a young man named Ferdinand wanders about, Ariel the spirit follows him and sings into his ear. In the song, Ariel tells Ferdinand that his father has died in the wreck. Of course, this isn't true; it's just part of Prospero's grand scheme. The song that Ariel sings is the poem students are about to read.

Build Vocabulary

Some words in this poem have changed in meaning since Shakespeare's time, and other words have fallen out of use. Explain these words to students. Students may also see the definitions of these words on the second activity page.

doth: does

fade: disintegrate, dissolve

fathom: a unit of measurement equal to six feet

knell: bell, gong

rich: ornate, intricate

sea-nymph: mermaid

suffer: undergo

thy: your

While You Read the Poem

Remind students that this poem was intended to be sung. Invite volunteers to take turns reading the poem aloud while keeping this in mind. Encourage students to make up their own simple melody for the song.

After You Read the Poem

Elements of Poetry

Form: Rhyming Verse Ask students to tell you whether this poem is free verse or rhyming. Verify that it is rhyming verse, and then ask students to help you identify the rhyming pairs of words, which are *lies, eyes; made, fade; sea-change, strange;* and *knell, bell.*

Poet's Toolbox: Word Order In English, basic sentence structure begins with a subject, followed by a verb and a complement. Poets love to play and experiment with this order. In this poem, for example, the line "Full fathom five thy father lies" is the reverse of how we would say it in "normal" English: "Thy father lies five full fathoms" (beneath the ocean). Ask students to similarly change the word order in the rest of the poem. Students will also have an opportunity to do this on the second activity page.

Follow-up Activities

Students may work independently to complete the activities on pages 89 and 90.

Full Fathom Five

Full fathom five thy father lies.
 Of his bones are coral made;
Those are pearls that were his eyes;
 Nothing of him that doth fade
But doth suffer a sea-change
Into something rich and strange.
Sea-nymphs hourly ring his knell:
 Hark, now I hear them.
 Ding-dong bell.

—*William Shakespeare*

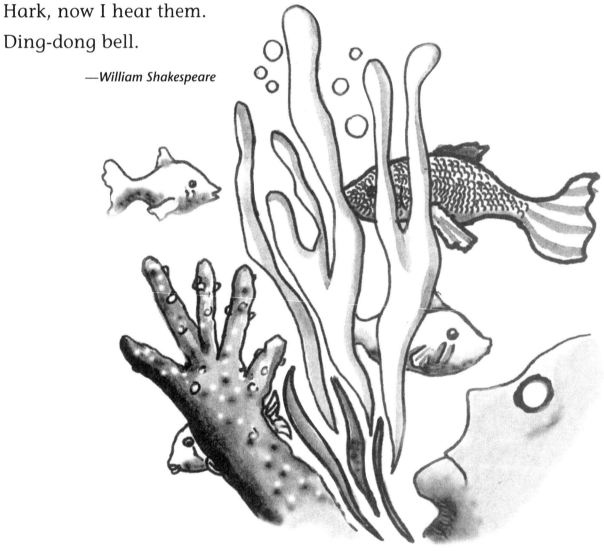

Did You Know? This poem is from a play called *The Tempest*. In the play, a spirit named Ariel sings this song to a castaway. Ariel wants him to think that his father has drowned in the ocean, even though it's not true. The castaway is spooked by the song and believes it.

Full Fathom Five

Understanding the Poem

Read each question and choose the best answer. You may wish to reread
"Full Fathom Five" as you work.

1. The speaker in the poem is describing the father as _____.
   - Ⓐ drowned
   - Ⓑ lost at sea
   - Ⓒ a sea creature
   - Ⓓ looking for his son

2. If a fathom is six feet, the distance in the first line is _____.
   - Ⓐ one mile
   - Ⓑ thirty feet
   - Ⓒ thirty-five feet
   - Ⓓ too far to measure

3. The "pearls" and "coral" are really _____.
   - Ⓐ teeth and nails
   - Ⓑ eyes and bones
   - Ⓒ nowhere to be seen
   - Ⓓ washed up on shore

4. The word *suffer* in the fifth line is used to mean _____.
   - Ⓐ cry
   - Ⓑ change
   - Ⓒ fade away
   - Ⓓ go through

5. The sea-nymphs seem to be doing some kind of _____.
   - Ⓐ chore
   - Ⓑ rescue
   - Ⓒ funeral service
   - Ⓓ song and dance

Full Fathom Five

Understanding the Poem

The way that Shakespeare used some of the words in this poem might be new to you. Study this list.

doth: does   **hark:** listen   **sea-nymph:** mermaid

fade: dissolve, disintegrate   **knell:** bell, gong   **suffer:** go through, experience

fathom: six feet deep   **rich:** ornate, intricate, detailed   **thy:** your

1. Use the definitions to write each line of the poem in "normal" English. To do that, you will have to change the word order.

   Example:

   Full fathom five your father lies = ____Your father lies thirty feet____ ____below the ocean's surface.____

   Of his bones are coral made = _____ _____

   _____

   Those are pearls that were his eyes = _____

   _____

   Nothing of him that doth fade = _____   ← **HINT #1:** Try changing *nothing* to *everything* or *every part.*

   _____

   But doth suffer a sea-change = _____   ← **HINT #2:** If you followed Hint #1, you should now change *but* to *and.*

   _____

   Into something rich and strange = _____ _____

   _____

2. Now, change the poem into a short speech, using your answers from above. Feel free to make more changes if you'd like.

   _____

   _____

   _____

   _____

From the Pages of History

Contents

Before You Read the Poem

Build Background

Tell students that the poems in this unit are about important moments in American history. The poem they will read next is called "The Landlord's Tale," but most people know it by the title of "Paul Revere's Ride." It was written by the famous American poet Henry Wadsworth Longfellow. Students may remember his poem "The Village Blacksmith" (see page 51). The poet's grandfather fought in the Revolutionary War, but when Longfellow wrote this poem, the country was on the brink of a different conflict: the Civil War. Longfellow wanted to remind Americans of the vision of the Founding Fathers and show them that the courage of one person could make a difference.

Build Vocabulary

Encourage students to give meanings for these words and phrases. Introduce any unfamiliar words.

aloft: high up

barrack: a building that houses soldiers

belfry: bell tower

impetuous: impulsive

muffled: a dulled or deadened sound

muster: to gather soldiers for roll call

phantom: ghost, something without substance

sentinel: a guard or watchman

spar: a wood piece that supports the rigging for a sail

spectral: ghostly

somber: solemn, sad, dark

steed: horse

tread: footstep

While You Read the Poem

If possible, take time before class to read through the poem yourself (aloud, if possible). For a first reading with the class, invite students to listen as you present an engaging reading of the poem. Afterwards, assign stanzas to small groups, and then conduct an ensemble "performance" of the poem. Students may be motivated to memorize some or all of this lengthy poem, especially if they are invited to present it at a school assembly, for a parent gathering, or for a class "democracy day" or "freedom celebration."

After You Read the Poem

Elements of Poetry

Form: Narrative Verse Remind students that narrative verse tells a story—in this case, one based on historical events. Narrative poetry is part of an ancient tradition of oral narration. These poems are meant to be spoken aloud and listened to. Encourage students to feel the strong meter that helps move the poem along, captures the excitement of the ride, and makes for interesting listening.

Follow-up Activities

Students may work independently to complete the activities on pages 97 and 98.

The Landlord's Tale: Paul Revere's Ride

1 Listen, my children, and you shall hear
Of the midnight ride of Paul Revere,
On the eighteenth of April, in Seventy-five;
Hardly a man is now alive
Who remembers that famous day and year.

2 He said to his friend, "If the British march
By land or sea from the town to-night,
Hang a lantern aloft in the belfry arch
Of the North Church tower, as a signal light,—
One, if by land, and two, if by sea;
And I on the opposite shore will be,
Ready to ride and spread the alarm
Through every Middlesex village and farm,
For the country folk to be up and to arm."

3 Then he said "Good-night!" and with muffled oar
Silently rowed to the Charlestown shore,
Just as the moon rose over the bay,
Where swinging wide at her moorings lay
The Somerset, British man-of-war;
A phantom ship, with each mast and spar
Across the moon like a prison bar,
And a huge black hulk, that was magnified
By its own reflection in the tide.

4 Meanwhile, his friend through alley and street
Wanders and watches, with eager ears,
Till in the silence around him he hears
The muster of men at the barrack door,
The sound of arms, and the tramp of feet,
And the measured tread of the grenadiers,
Marching down to their boats on the shore.

5 Then he climbed the tower of the Old North Church,
   By the wooden stairs, with stealthy tread,
   To the belfry chamber overhead,
   And startled the pigeons from their perch
   On the sombre rafters, that round him made
   Masses and moving shapes of shade,—
   By the trembling ladder, steep and tall,
   To the highest window in the wall,
   Where he paused to listen and look down
   A moment on the roofs of the town,
   And the moonlight flowing over all.

6 Beneath, in the churchyard, lay the dead,
   In their night encampment on the hill,
   Wrapped in silence so deep and still
   That he could hear, like a sentinel's tread,
   The watchful night-wind, as it went
   Creeping along from tent to tent,
   And seeming to whisper, "All is well!"
   A moment only he feels the spell
   Of the place and the hour, and the secret dread
   Of the lonely belfry and the dead;
   For suddenly all his thoughts are bent
   On a shadowy something far away,
   Where the river widens to meet the bay,—
   A line of black that bends and floats
   On the rising tide like a bridge of boats.

7 Meanwhile, impatient to mount and ride,
   Booted and spurred, with a heavy stride
   On the opposite shore walked Paul Revere.
   Now he patted his horse's side,
   Now gazed on the landscape far and near,
   Then, impetuous, stamped the earth,
   And turned and tightened his saddle girth;
   But mostly he watched with eager search
   The belfry tower of the Old North Church,
   As it rose above the graves on the hill,
   Lonely and spectral and sombre and still.
   And lo! as he looks, on the belfry's height
   A glimmer, and then a gleam of light!
   He springs to the saddle, the bridle he turns,
   But lingers and gazes, till full on his sight
   A second lamp in the belfry burns!

      Read and Understand Poetry • EMC 3325 • ©2005 by Evan-Moor Corp.

8   A hurry of hoofs in a village street,
    A shape in the moonlight, a bulk in the dark,
    And beneath, from the pebbles, in passing, a spark
    Struck out by a steed flying fearless and fleet;
    That was all! And yet, through the gloom and the light,
    The fate of a nation was riding that night;
    And the spark struck out by that steed, in his flight,
    Kindled the land into flame with its heat.

9   He has left the village and mounted the steep,
    And beneath him, tranquil and broad and deep,
    Is the Mystic, meeting the ocean tides;
    And under the alders that skirt its edge,
    Now soft on the sand, now loud on the ledge,
    Is heard the tramp of his steed as he rides.

10 It was twelve by the village clock
    When he crossed the bridge into Medford town.
    He heard the crowing of the cock,
    And the barking of the farmer's dog,
    And felt the damp of the river fog,
    That rises after the sun goes down.

11 It was one by the village clock,
    When he galloped into Lexington.
    He saw the gilded weathercock
    Swim in the moonlight as he passed,
    And the meeting-house windows, black and bare,
    Gaze at him with a spectral glare,
    As if they already stood aghast
    At the bloody work they would look upon.

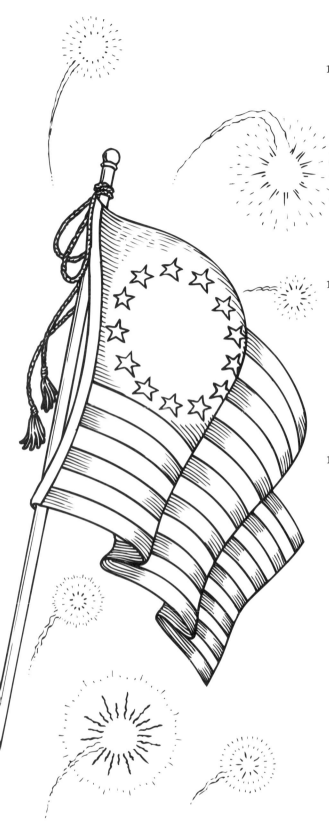

12 It was two by the village clock,
    When be came to the bridge in Concord town.
    He heard the bleating of the flock,
    And the twitter of birds among the trees,
    And felt the breath of the morning breeze
    Blowing over the meadow brown.
    And one was safe and asleep in his bed
    Who at the bridge would be first to fall,
    Who that day would be lying dead,
    Pierced by a British musket ball.

13 You know the rest. In the books you have read
    How the British Regulars fired and fled,—
    How the farmers gave them ball for ball,
    From behind each fence and farm-yard wall,
    Chasing the redcoats down the lane,
    Then crossing the fields to emerge again
    Under the trees at the turn of the road,
    And only pausing to fire and load.

14 So through the night rode Paul Revere;
    And so through the night went his cry of alarm
    To every Middlesex village and farm,—
    A cry of defiance, and not of fear,
    A voice in the darkness, a knock at the door,
    And a word that shall echo for evermore!
    For, borne on the night-wind of the Past,
    Through all our history, to the last,
    In the hour of darkness and peril and need,
    The people will waken and listen to hear
    The hurrying hoof-beats of that steed,
    And the midnight message of Paul Revere.

—*Henry Wadsworth Longfellow*

Did You Know? Although this poem is based on historical events, Longfellow has made some creative changes to the true story. To learn more about these famous events, you may wish to read *Paul Revere's Ride* by David Hackett Fischer. Or, check out the beautiful and informative presentation by illustrator Christopher Bing in *The Midnight Ride of Paul Revere.*

Understanding the Poem

Read each question and choose the best answer. You may wish to reread "The Landlord's Tale: Paul Revere's Ride" as you work.

1. Which of these is <u>not</u> mentioned in "The Landlord's Tale"?
    - Ⓐ the Mystic River
    - Ⓑ his friend's name
    - Ⓒ pigeons in the belfry
    - Ⓓ the Old North Church

2. "The Landlord's Tale" is mainly about _____.
    - Ⓐ Paul Revere's friend climbing up into the church bell tower
    - Ⓑ the British rowing on the river in the middle of the night
    - Ⓒ the patriots who fought in the Revolution
    - Ⓓ Paul Revere riding to warn the patriots

3. The "grenadiers" in stanza 4 are probably _____.
    - Ⓐ farmers
    - Ⓑ lawyers
    - Ⓒ soldiers
    - Ⓓ teachers

4. According to "The Landlord's Tale," _____.
    - Ⓐ British soldiers took Paul Revere's horse
    - Ⓑ Paul Revere rode all the way to Concord
    - Ⓒ Paul Revere only got as far as Lexington
    - Ⓓ Paul Revere was not the only rider that night

5. Climbing the ladder to the bell tower must have been _____.
    - Ⓐ easy
    - Ⓑ tedious
    - Ⓒ delightful
    - Ⓓ frightening

Understanding the Poem

1. "Paul Revere's Ride" is a narrative poem. It tells a story, and is meant to be recited. A strong pattern of accented and unaccented syllables helps create a steady meter. This makes it easier to feel the rhyme pattern in the poem and to recite it. Look at the way the meter is marked in this section of the poem.

Lísten, my chíldren, and yóu shall héar
Of the mídnight ríde of Paúl Revére,
On the eíghteenth of Ápril, in Séventy-Fíve;
Hárdly a mán is nów alíve
Who remémbers that fámous daý and yeár.

Copy another section of the poem below. Mark the pattern of stressed and unstressed syllables using accent marks as in the example above.

_____

_____

_____

_____

_____

2. The pattern of rhyme for the first stanza of the poem is *aabba*. What is the pattern of rhyme for the section of the poem that you wrote above? Put the same letter at the end of lines that rhyme, and a different letter for other rhyme patterns. Write your pattern here:

_____

3. History tells us that at least two other riders warned the patriots that night. Do you think Longfellow should have included them in the poem? Why or why not?

_____

_____

_____

_____

Before You Read the Poem

Build Background

Ask students to share what they know about the Underground Railroad. If necessary, explain that the Underground Railroad was a secret system of escape for enslaved African Americans. It began in response to the Fugitive Slave Act, and was active mainly from 1830 to 1860. "Conductors" led escaped slaves in small groups through the wilderness toward Canada. Most of the conductors were African American, but white Americans who were sympathetic to their plight often provided safe havens for short periods of time. This underground system, due to its extreme secrecy, was always changing, and people participated to different degrees for varying lengths of time. Some members coordinated their efforts with others in elaborate and ongoing operations, but others acted on their own, offering help on a much smaller scale whenever it was possible. This poem tells about an encounter between a white man and a fugitive slave that doesn't seem to be connected to the Underground Railroad in a direct sense, although it emerges from that context.

While You Read the Poem

Invite a few volunteers to take turns reading the poem aloud for the class. Tell students that they should read the poem in the same way they would tell a story; the poem is, in fact, written as a personal reminiscence.

After You Read the Poem

Elements of Poetry

Form: Narrative Verse This poem tells a short story of sorts. Like all stories, it has a setting, characters, and a plot. Ask students to help you identify these elements. Point out that the final line appears out of order—in that line, the speaker tells how he and the fugitive ate together at the same table, but the slave has already left the house, as described in the previous line. The final line is presented as an afterthought to give the reader a further glimpse into the story and the nature of the exchange between the two characters.

Poet's Toolbox: Atmosphere Talk with students about the tools and techniques the poet used to create the quiet, intimate atmosphere of this poem. The setting, for example, seems to be in a remote place, away from town, accentuating the sense of privacy. The poet also describes a number of sounds and other details that aren't usually noticed in a noisy, bustling environment. His awareness of the runaway's "revolving eyes," also shows that he is attuned to the man's feelings and emotions. The firearm in the last line is a reminder that the two are in great danger, a detail that enhances the atmosphere of tension behind the quiet.

Follow-up Activities

Students may work independently to complete the activities on pages 101 and 102.

The Runaway Slave

The runaway slave came to my house and stopt outside,

I heard his motions crackling the twigs of the woodpile,

Through the swung half-door of the kitchen I saw him
limpsy and weak,

And went where he sat on a log and led him in and
assured him,

And brought water and fill'd a tub for his sweated body
and bruis'd feet,

And gave him a room that enter'd from my own, and
gave him some coarse clean clothes,

And remember perfectly well his revolving eyes and
his awkwardness,

And remember putting plasters on the galls of his neck
and ankles;

He staid with me a week before he was recuperated and
pass'd north,

I had him sit next me at table, my fire-lock lean'd in the corner.

—*Walt Whitman*

Read and Understand Poetry • EMC 3325 • ©2005 by Evan-Moor Corp.

Understanding the Poem

Read each question and choose the best answer. You may wish to reread
"The Runaway Slave" as you work.

1. The slave in this poem has _____.
   - Ⓐ broken no laws
   - Ⓑ made it to Canada
   - Ⓒ bought his own freedom
   - Ⓓ escaped and is on the run

2. The runaway stayed for a whole week because _____.
   - Ⓐ he was weak and injured
   - Ⓑ his family was trying to find him
   - Ⓒ he had arrived at his destination
   - Ⓓ the white man asked him for his help

3. You can tell this poem takes place _____.
   - Ⓐ during the 1900s
   - Ⓑ right after the Civil War
   - Ⓒ before slavery was abolished
   - Ⓓ at a time when it was illegal to own slaves

4. The "fire-lock" in the last line must be _____.
   - Ⓐ a code word
   - Ⓑ a rifle or shotgun
   - Ⓒ some kind of match
   - Ⓓ the grate in front of the fireplace

5. The narrator of this poem was probably the kind of person who _____.
   - Ⓐ always obeyed the law
   - Ⓑ didn't think for himself
   - Ⓒ had no sense of right or wrong
   - Ⓓ broke rules when he thought it was the right thing to do

Name _____

The Runaway Slave

Understanding the Poem

1. This poem tells a kind of story. Place these events from the poem in the order they happened.

    _____ He asked the runaway to come indoors.

    _____ The man who lived there came outside.

    _____ The man gave the runaway some clothes and a place to sleep.

    _____ They ate dinner together.

    _____ After seven days, the runaway could walk once again.

    _____ The owner of the house brought the runaway water to bathe in.

    ___1___ A runaway slave stopped by a cabin in the woods.

    _____ He continued on his way north after he was stronger.

    _____ The man in the cabin tended to the runaway's injuries.

2. Write a short story based on these events. You may use the sentences above, but feel free to make changes and add your own details.

    _____

    _____

    _____

    _____

    _____

    _____

    _____

    _____

    _____

    _____

    _____

Read and Understand Poetry • EMC 3325 • ©2005 by Evan-Moor Corp.

Before You Read the Poem

Build Background

With students, review what the class has learned from the previous lesson about slavery and the Underground Railroad. You might also provide some additional information about the Fugitive Slave Act of 1850. There were several versions of this law, but the basic provision was that fugitive slaves could be forcibly returned to their masters, even if they had made it to a free state in the North. For this reason, Canada was the ultimate destination for many fugitives. This poem tells about the hardships that fugitive slaves had to endure.

While You Read the Poem

Because this poem has fifteen stanzas, assign one stanza to fifteen different students. If there are fewer than fifteen students in your class, have each student read two or more stanzas.

After You Read the Poem

Elements of Poetry

Form: Ode A poem that uses exalted language to celebrate a particular subject is called an *ode*. In "The Fugitive," the poet pays tribute to the strength and perseverance of those slaves who fled bondage in search of freedom. More specifically, the poet is celebrating the fortitude of fugitive black men who braved incredible hardships while they were "underground," or on the run. During the slave era, many slave owners tried to make black men feel like they were less than true men. They did this in many ways, but especially by making it impossible for them to protect and provide for their families. Here, the poet dispels the image of inferiority and instead pays homage to the brave men of her race that she so clearly admires and respects. Ask students to find the words and phrases that the poet uses to show her respect for fugitive slaves.

Poet's Toolbox: Meter Explain to students that meter is the way in which we measure the rhythm of poetry. The basic unit of measurement is called a *foot*. A metrical foot usually consists of two syllables (but sometimes three). Have students determine the meter of this poem by first asking them to count the number of syllables in a line, and then divide by two. For example, the first line in this poem has eight syllables; it therefore is made up of four feet. The second line has three feet. The last two lines in the stanza repeat this pattern. Each stanza in the poem follows the same meter, which is typical of an ode.

Follow-up Activities

Students may work independently to complete the activities on pages 106 and 107.

The Fugitive

1 With bleeding back, from tyrant's lash,
   A fleet-foot slave has sped,
   All frantic, past his humble hut,
   And seeks the wood instead.

2 Once in the woods, his manhood wakes;
   Why stand this bondage, wroth?
   With diabolic, reckless heart,
   He turns he, to the North.

3 He flings his crude hat to the ground,
   And face the northern wind;
   Fleet in his tracks, the blood-hounds bay,
   He leaves them far behind.

4 By devious way, cross many a stream,
   He fiercely pressed that day,
   With deadly oaths for brush or brake,
   That chance to block his way.

5 Erelong, when kind and soothing night,
   Had hushed the strife of man,
   He wades waist-deep, unto a tree,
   To rest awhile and plan.

6 He knows no friends or shelter, kind,
   To soothe his deadly grief,
   He only knows, that farther north,
   A slave may find relief.

7 No lore of book, or college crafts,
   Lends cunning to his plan,
   Fresh from the tyrant's blasting touch.
   He stands a crude, rough, man.

   Read and Understand Poetry • EMC 3325 • ©2005 by Evan-Moor Corp.

8   But Providence, with pity, deep,
    Looked down upon that slave,
    And mapped a path, up through the South,
    And strength and courage gave.

9   Sometimes, a friendly fellow-slave,
    Chance, spying where he hid,
    At night would bring his coarse, rough, fare,
    And God-speed warmly bid.

10 And sometimes, when to hunger fierce,
    He's seem almost to yield,
    A bird would fall into his clutch,
    A fish would shake his reel.

11 And when on reaching colder climes,
    A sheep-cote shelter made,
    Or, law-abiding Yankee, stern,
    Clandestinely, lent aid.

12 Till after many a restless day,
    And weary, toiling, night,
    All foot-sore, worn, and tired of limb,
    His haven looms in sight.

13 His tired feet press Canadian shore,
    Friends tell him he is free;
    He feels a craving still, to hide,
    It seems it cannot be.

14 But from suspense and thralldom freed,
    His manhood wakes at last,
    And plies he hand and brain with might,
    To mend his ruthless past.

15 And Providence, in years that came,
    Sent blessings rife, his way,
    With grateful heart journeyed through,
    His free, allotted days.

                        —*Priscilla Jane Thompson*

From the Pages of History

The Fugitive

Understanding the Poem

Read each question and choose the best answer. You may wish to reread "The Fugitive" as you work.

1. This poem tells mainly about slaves that _____.
   - Ⓐ fight back against slavery
   - Ⓑ wait patiently for their freedom
   - Ⓒ have escaped and are on the run
   - Ⓓ try to make the best of their situation

2. In this poem, the fugitive relies mainly on _____.
   - Ⓐ his own wits
   - Ⓑ friendly white people
   - Ⓒ charity and sympathy
   - Ⓓ other fugitives he meets along the way

3. The fugitive made it all the way to _____.
   - Ⓐ Mexico
   - Ⓑ Canada
   - Ⓒ Boston, Massachusetts
   - Ⓓ Providence, Rhode Island

4. The fugitive's trip was _____.
   - Ⓐ all in vain
   - Ⓑ too dangerous to complete
   - Ⓒ worth all the risks he took
   - Ⓓ a lot easier than he thought it would be

5. You can tell that the poet _____.
   - Ⓐ is proud of her race
   - Ⓑ feels anger over the past
   - Ⓒ was never a slave herself
   - Ⓓ doesn't have very much hope for the future

The Fugitive

Understanding the Poem

Do you know all of the words in the poem? This exercise will help you understand them. Match each word or phrase from the box with one of the words in boldface. Write the word on the line.

backroads	climate	continued	fear
give in	good fortune	in abundance	quick
secretly	sense of pride	trap	whip

With bleeding back, from tyrant's **lash**,   _____

A **fleet-foot** slave has sped,   _____

By **devious way**, cross many a stream,   _____

He fiercely **pressed** that day,   _____

And sometimes, when to hunger fierce,

He's seem almost to **yield**,   _____

A bird would fall into his **clutch**,   _____

A fish would shake his reel.

And when on reaching colder **climes**,   _____

A sheep-cote shelter made,

Or, law-abiding Yankee, stern,

Clandestinely, lent aid.   _____

But from suspense and **thralldom** freed,   _____

His **manhood** wakes at last,   _____

And **Providence**, in years that came,   _____

Sent blessings **rife**, his way,   _____

From the Pages of History

Before You Read the Poem

Build Background

Remind students that the poems in this unit are about important moments in American history. This poem, called "The New Colossus," was written in 1883 by Emma Lazarus, a Jewish American poet and essayist. She wrote it to help raise money for the pedestal of the Statue of Liberty. The poem is engraved on a plaque at the entrance to the pedestal. It is called "The New Colossus" because the Statue of Liberty is similar to another big statue created for a harbor. The Colossus of Rhodes, one of the Seven Wonders of the Ancient World, was a huge figure that was meant to scare people away from the harbor it guarded. The Statue of Liberty, however, has been a symbol of welcome to immigrants from around the world who first arrived by ship at New York's harbor.

Build Vocabulary

Encourage students to give meanings for these words and phrases. Explain any that are unfamiliar.

astride: legs apart, one leg on each side of something

brazen: bold, filled with contempt

Colossus: a giant statue

conquering: defeating an enemy, winning

exiles: people driven out of their homeland

refuse: trash, discards

storied: written about in stories, legendary

tempest: storm

yearning: longing, wanting

While You Read the Poem

Invite students to read through the poem silently one or two times, and then ask a volunteer to read it aloud for the class. Students may enjoy hearing the poem read aloud several times by different readers.

After You Read the Poem

Elements of Poetry

Form: Sonnet Tell students that this poem is a sonnet. It has fourteen lines that are divided into two parts. The first eight lines, also called an *octave,* describe the statue; this part has a rhyme scheme of *abbaabba*. In the final six lines, or *sestet,* the statue speaks. The rhyme scheme is *cdcdcd*.

Follow-up Activities

Students may work independently to complete the activities on pages 110 and 111.

The New Colossus

Not like the brazen giant of Greek fame,
With conquering limbs astride from land to land;
Here at our sea-washed, sunset gates shall stand
A mighty woman with a torch, whose flame
Is the imprisoned lightning, and her name
Mother of Exiles. From her beacon-hand
Glows world-wide welcome; her mild eyes command
The air-bridged harbor that twin cities frame.
"Keep, ancient lands, your storied pomp!" cries she
With silent lips. "Give me your tired, your poor,
Your huddled masses yearning to breathe free,
The wretched refuse of your teeming shore.
Send these, the homeless, tempest-tost to me,
I lift my lamp beside the golden door!"

—*Emma Lazarus*

Understanding the Poem

Read each question and choose the best answer. You may wish to reread "The New Colossus" as you work.

1. Which of these is mentioned first in "The New Colossus"?
   - Ⓐ the golden door
   - Ⓑ New York Harbor
   - Ⓒ the Mother of Exiles
   - Ⓓ the original Colossus

2. "The New Colossus" is mainly about _____ .
   - Ⓐ a brazen giant
   - Ⓑ imprisoned lightning
   - Ⓒ the Statue of Liberty
   - Ⓓ the air-bridged harbor

3. The word *wretched* probably means _____ .
   - Ⓐ miserable
   - Ⓑ attractive
   - Ⓒ talented
   - Ⓓ wealthy

4. How does the statue feel about the Old World's achievements?
   - Ⓐ She is envious of them.
   - Ⓑ She wants to copy them.
   - Ⓒ She is impressed by them.
   - Ⓓ She is not impressed by them.

5. What is the "beacon-hand"?
   - Ⓐ a visitor waving from the top
   - Ⓑ the uplifted hand with a torch
   - Ⓒ a lighthouse built into the statue
   - Ⓓ the men who delivered the statue

Name _____

Understanding the Poem

1. Synonyms are words that have the same meaning. Write a synonym for each of these words from the poem. Use a dictionary or thesaurus if you need to.

conquering _____

storied _____

refuse _____

wretched _____

huddled _____

tempest _____

yearning _____

2. "The New Colossus" is a sonnet. It follows a pattern of rhyme. Find words in the poem that rhyme with each of the words below and write them on the lines. Some of the rhymes are not exact, but close. These are called *near rhymes*. Include them in the lists, too.

fame	land	she	poor
flame	_____	_____	_____
_____	_____	_____	_____
_____	_____		

3. According to the poem, how is the Statue of Liberty different from the Colossus of Rhodes, "the brazen giant of Greek fame"?

_____

_____

4. What is the poet talking about when she mentions "golden door" in the last line of the poem?

_____

_____

Celebrate!

Contents

Read and Understand Poetry • EMC 3325 • ©2005 by Evan-Moor Corp.

Before You Read the Poem

Build Background

With students, conduct a discussion about Chinese New Year festivities. Include the following information: The Chinese New Year is celebrated in late January or early February. In Chinese communities around the world, the year begins with a colorful parade. A major highlight of the parade is a dragon, which symbolizes good luck. Firecrackers are also set off to bring good luck and scare away bad spirits. Invite students to share about a Chinese New Year's parade they have attended or seen on television.

Build Vocabulary

Ask students to brainstorm words that tell about the sights, sounds, smells, and tastes of a Chinese New Year Parade. Record their suggestions in a simple graphic organizer.

While You Read the Poem

Form four groups of students. Assign one of the four stanzas to each group. Then have groups chorally read their assigned stanzas in order.

After You Read the Poem

Elements of Poetry

Form: Rhyming Verse Point out the rhyming words *Town* and *down* in the first stanza. Remind students that poets usually establish a rhyming pattern in the first stanza and then stick to that pattern throughout the poem. The rhyming pattern of the first stanza of this poem could be represented as *abcb* because *Day* and *year* in the first and third lines do not rhyme. Ask students to confirm that the poet follows this pattern in each of the successive stanzas (which he does).

Poet's Toolbox: Stressed and Unstressed Syllables Explain to students that a poem's rhythm is the beat established by the pattern of stressed and unstressed syllables. Demonstrate by clapping on the stressed syllables of the first stanza: "It's Néw Year's Dáy/in Chína Tówn/anóther yeár/is cóunted dówn." Have students join in with you. You may want to write the first stanza on the board to model how to mark the stressed syllables. Students will further explore these stress patterns on the second activity page.

Follow-up Activities

Students may work independently to complete the activities on pages 115 and 116.

Chinese New Year in China Town

It's New Year's Day
in China Town,
another year
is counted down.

Fireworks shoot
showers of light
lanterns wave,
burning bright.

Children dance
in the crowd,
smiling faces
cheer out loud.

Dragons twist
up and down,
for it's New Year's Day
in China Town.

—Andrew Collett

Read and Understand Poetry • EMC 3325 • ©2005 by Evan-Moor Corp.

Name _____

Understanding the Poem

Read each question and choose the best answer. You may wish to reread
"Chinese New Year in China Town" as you work.

1. The parade described in the poem includes _____.

   Ⓐ torches
   Ⓑ cheering dragons
   Ⓒ lanterns and fireworks
   Ⓓ a lion dance and acrobats

2. In the poem, the new year is counted down and then _____.

   Ⓐ lanterns are lit
   Ⓑ fireworks go off
   Ⓒ children dance
   Ⓓ people cheer out loud

3. In the last stanza, "for it's New Year's Day" means _____.

   Ⓐ just in time
   Ⓑ for the first time
   Ⓒ because it's New Year's Day
   Ⓓ before New Year's Day arrives

4. In the Chinese culture, dragons are probably _____.

   Ⓐ good luck
   Ⓑ a bad sign
   Ⓒ as real as any other animal
   Ⓓ traditional fairy tale characters

5. The Chinese New Year's Day parade is _____.

   Ⓐ a scary time
   Ⓑ a happy time
   Ⓒ a time for bonfires
   Ⓓ a time for showers

Name _____

Understanding the Poem

Read the poem aloud and listen for the stressed syllables. Make a mark above each stressed syllable. The first stanza has been done for you. Do you notice a pattern?

It's Néw Year's Dáy
in Chína Tówn,
anóther yeár
is cóunted dówn.

Fireworks shoot
showers of light
lanterns wave,
burning bright.

Children dance
in the crowd,
smiling faces
cheer out loud.

Dragons twist
up and down,
for it's New Year's Day
in China Town.

Before You Read the Poem

Build Background

Remind students that the poems in this chapter are about celebrations. Tell students that the poem they will read next is called "New Year Prayer." It is about Rosh Hashanah, the Jewish New Year celebration. Rosh Hashanah is considered "the birthday of creation" and begins with the blast of the *shofar,* or ram's horn. If any students celebrate Rosh Hashanah, invite them to share their traditions. These might include eating special foods, such as apples dipped in honey to ensure a sweet year and bread shaped in a spiral as a reminder that the cycle of the year goes 'round and 'round, year after year.

Build Vocabulary

Encourage students to give meanings for the following words and phrases. Present the meaning of any terms that are unfamiliar.

harmony: two or more elements fitting together in a pleasing or peaceful way

humanity: all human beings; the quality of being human; compassion

renewal: the act of making something new or fresh again

spirit: life force, essence

While You Read the Poem

Invite students to read through the poem silently. Choose a different student to read each line aloud. Explain that in music, a *rest* is a planned space of silence. In many poems, commas and periods serve as rests, but in some poems, such as this one, there is no punctuation. Ask students where pauses could be included. Have volunteers read the poem with pauses in different places.

After You Read the Poem

Elements of Poetry

Form: Acrostic Explain that some poems are written to include extra meanings that cannot be heard when the poem is read aloud because they appear only in print. In an acrostic poem, a word or short message is spelled out by the first letter of each line. This message is always related to the theme of the poem. Invite students to discover what is spelled by the first letter of each line in "New Year Prayer."

Poet's Toolbox: Phraseology A phrase is a cluster of related words. Sometimes, a poet conveys a great deal of meaning through a simple phrase, even though the phrase does not form a complete sentence. In this poem, the poet has strung together a list of values and concepts that are all related to the spirit of Rosh Hashanah. Invite students to experiment with different ways of grouping the words into phrases. They will also be asked to do so on the second activity page.

Follow-up Activities

Students may work independently to complete the activities on pages 119 and 120.

New Year Prayer

Renewal

Of

Spirit

Healing

Heart

And

Soul

Harmony

Among

Nations

And

Humanity

—*Sarita Chávez Silverman*

 Did You Know? Rosh Hashanah, the Jewish New Year, always begins on the first day of the Jewish month of Tishrei. In 2001, this date corresponded to Tuesday, September 18 on the Gregorian calendar (the calendar used in the United States and much of the world). This date was exactly one week after the events of September 11, 2001. This poem expresses the poet's hopes for healing and forgiveness following the tragic events of that day.

Understanding the Poem

Read each question and choose the best answer. You may wish to reread "New Year Prayer" as you work.

1. Which of these is <u>not</u> mentioned in the poem?
   - Ⓐ harmony among nations
   - Ⓑ renewal of spirit
   - Ⓒ hopes and fears
   - Ⓓ heart and soul

2. Which of these is mentioned last in the poem?
   - Ⓐ humanity
   - Ⓑ renewal
   - Ⓒ healing
   - Ⓓ heart

3. The word *soul* in the poem probably means _____.
   - Ⓐ part of a shoe
   - Ⓑ a type of food
   - Ⓒ a type of music
   - Ⓓ a person's spirit

4. This poem is <u>not</u> about _____.
   - Ⓐ a fresh start
   - Ⓑ building a temple
   - Ⓒ the Jewish New Year
   - Ⓓ a prayer for peace and harmony

5. Which of these kinds of thoughts are best to keep in mind on Rosh Hashanah?
   - Ⓐ selfish and greedy
   - Ⓑ fearful and nervous
   - Ⓒ hopeful and positive
   - Ⓓ sad and discouraged

Understanding the Poem

1. The prefix *re-* means "to make or do again." The word *renew* means "to make new again." Write the meaning of these words that have the prefix *re-*.

rewrite _____

reappear _____

review_____

2. The poet could have included punctuation in this poem. Why do you think she left it out?

_____

_____

3. Draw a line to connect each word with its meaning.

harmony   all human beings

spirit   a pleasing combination

humanity   life force

4. Remember that when words in a poem begin with the same consonant sounds, it is called *alliteration*. In "New Year's Prayer," four words begin with an *h* sound. What are they?

_____   _____

_____   _____

5. In the last line of the poem, the word *humanity* can mean several things. Circle all of the possible meanings.

all humans   all living things   human caring   compassion

6. The words in the poem may be read as three phrases. What are they?

_____

_____

_____

Before You Read the Poem

Build Background

Tell students that they are going to read a poem about an Indian holiday called Diwali, also known as "the festival of lights." It is celebrated on the 15th day of the Hindu month of Ashwin, which usually falls toward the end of October or the beginning of November. This is the night of the new moon, and it is one of the darkest nights of the year. During the night of Diwali, Hindus light small earthen lamps called *diyas*. They are arranged on altars dedicated to deities and other auspicious figures such as Lakshmi, the goddess of wealth and prosperity; Lord Rama, the hero of an Indian epic called the *Ramayana*; and his wife, Sita. By observing these rituals, Hindus are assured that the coming year will be full of joy and abundance. Diwali is celebrated in Hindu communities throughout the world, including India, Thailand, Trinidad, Malaysia, and the United States, to name just a few.

While You Read the Poem

Lead the class in a choral reading of the poem. You might want to "direct," like a conductor, to help establish the rhythm of the poem. Afterward, invite one or two volunteers to take turns leading the class in another choral reading. Encourage them to look at themselves as "conductors" of a choral recital.

After You Read the Poem

Elements of Poetry

Form: Couplets With students, search the poem for rhyming words. Be sure they notice how the rhyming pairs appear at the end of each line. Explain to students that pairs of rhyming lines are called *couplets*. Write the word on the board and ask them to find within it a more familiar word that means "two" *(couple)*. Work with students to identify the rhyming pattern in this poem, which is *aabbaaccddaa*.

Poet's Toolbox: Assonance and Alliteration The long *i* sound is echoed throughout the poem. It appears in rhyming pairs such as *light* and *night*, and in clusters such as "bright blazing light." The repetition of a vowel sound in key places throughout a poem is called *assonance*. Students may also recall that the repetition of initial consonants is called *alliteration;* this is also present in the repetitive phrase "bright blazing light." That phrase, therefore, does "double duty" because it is an example of both assonance and alliteration. Ask students to look for other examples of these techniques.

Follow-up Activities

Students may work independently to complete the activities on pages 123 and 124.

Diwali

Bright blazing light,
burning up the night
drive the dark and cold away
make the night-time bright as day
bright blazing light
beautiful sight
from each window lamps will burn
Rama, Sita will return
to bring us wealth, bring us love
from the goddess high above
bright blazing light
this Diwali night.

—*David Harmer*

Did You Know? *Diwali* is an important Hindu festival of light that falls during the dark days of winter. *Diwali* means "a row of lights." Oil-burning "diva lamps" are lit and fireworks are displayed for this festival. It is believed that light brings happiness and good luck, as do Rama and Sita, a couple viewed by Hindus as role models of ideal behavior. The "goddess high above" is Lakshmi, the goddess of abundance. During Diwali, she is believed to enter the homes of Hindus, bringing Rama and Sita with her.

Diwali

Understanding the Poem

Read each question and choose the best answer. You may wish to reread "Diwali" as you work.

1. Which of the following would <u>not</u> be in the spirit of the Diwali festival?
   - Ⓐ starting fresh
   - Ⓑ making resolutions
   - Ⓒ shining bright light into the darkness
   - Ⓓ meditating about troubles and problems

2. During this holiday, people _____.
   - Ⓐ hold contests
   - Ⓑ shoot fireworks
   - Ⓒ light candles and lamps
   - Ⓓ put money in envelopes

3. Rama and Sita must be associated with _____.
   - Ⓐ burning oil
   - Ⓑ good and evil
   - Ⓒ darkness and light
   - Ⓓ happiness and prosperity

4. You can tell from the poem that Rama and Sita _____.
   - Ⓐ are mortal enemies
   - Ⓑ are not related in any way
   - Ⓒ die when the lamps go out
   - Ⓓ live together in the heavens

5. According to the poem, lights are placed _____.
   - Ⓐ high above on rooftops
   - Ⓑ along the riverbank
   - Ⓒ on windowsills
   - Ⓓ down below

Name _____

Diwali

Understanding the Poem

1. *Alliteration* is when the same consonant letter appears at the beginning of two or more words that are close together, as in "the big blue yonder." The repetition of a vowel sound in phrases such as "free and easy" is called *assonance*. Review the following lines from the poem. Make a check in one or both columns to show if each line includes assonance, alliteration, both, or neither.

Line from Poem	Alliteration	Assonance
Bright, blazing light		
drive the dark and cold away		
make the night-time bright as day		
to bring us wealth, bring us love		
bright blazing light this Diwali night		

2. Use these words to write simple phrases that have alliteration.

blaze: _____

drive: _____

wealth: _____

3. Use the same words to write phrases with assonance.

blaze: _____

drive: _____

wealth: _____

4. Now, try to write phrases or sentences with both alliteration and assonance.

blaze: _____

drive: _____

wealth: _____

Read and Understand Poetry • EMC 3325 • ©2005 by Evan-Moor Corp.

Before You Read the Poem

Build Background

At the beginning of this unit, students read a poem about the Chinese New Year. In this lesson, students will read about Tuen Ng, another traditional Chinese celebration. It commemorates the death of Chu Yuan, a minister of state who was well known for his honesty and wisdom. Chu Yuan was an advisor to the King during the time of the Warring States (475–221 B.C.). Other advisors were jealous of Chu Yuan, and conspired against him. When power was handed over to a new king, Chu Yuan was sentenced to exile, but he instead jumped into a river. In a race against time, his friends and supporters paddled out to save him, but it was too late—Chu Yuan had drowned. On the fifth day of the fifth month of the Chinese calendar (early June), boat races are held in Chu Yuan's honor, which is why this holiday is also called the Dragon Boat Festival. In Hong Kong, thousands of spectators gather on the shore to picnic while watching the competition. This poem conveys what it's like to watch this colorful race.

While You Read the Poem

Invite a volunteer to read the poem aloud. When he or she comes to the second stanza, lead the rest of the class in a spirited choral reading of the lines: "And then . . . they're off! Away!" Students may also want to cheer and clap, as if they were witnessing the beginning of a race.

After You Read the Poem

Elements of Poetry

Form: Internal Rhyme When a poet uses words that rhyme in the same line of a poem, it is called *internal rhyme.* This technique can be used to strengthen the rhyming element of a poem that does not have a regular rhyming pattern. Ask students to read this poem to evaluate whether it follows a predictable pattern of rhyme (it does not). Then ask them to find the two examples of internal rhyme in the poem *(dip/whip* and *pumping/thumping).*

Poet's Toolbox: Comparative Devices This poem uses a variety of devices to compare and contrast images and ideas. With students, review the use of personification, similes, and metaphors, which they have learned about in previous lessons. Remind them of the following: personification is a way of giving human qualities to an animal, object, or idea; a metaphor is a comparison of two things that have some quality in common; a simile is also a comparison, but unlike a metaphor, it uses a signal word such as *like* or *as.* Ask students to find an example of each comparative device in the poem. They will have further practice doing this on the second activity page.

Follow-up Activities

Students may work independently to complete the activities on pages 127 and 128.

Tuen Ng—
The Dragon Boat Races

The air is hushed
round waiting boats;
water still before the race.
Slowly paddles lift
above the dragon-prows
like giant wing-bones
from a waking beast,
stretching into space. . .

And then. . . they're off!
Away!

Fish scatter in dismay
as dragon-racers slice the surface.
Wings dip, whip water into waves;
waves rise like flames,
set light by sun.

Above, flags tug at their fetters,
desperate to join the fun.
And all around,
like pumping, thumping dragon-hearts,
the pounding gongs,
the beating drum.

—Judith Nicholls

Did You Know? The Dragon Boat Race is a traditional Chinese holiday. It is held in rivers and waterfronts in Chinese communities around the world on the fifth day of the fifth month of the Chinese calendar, which usually falls in early June.

Read and Understand Poetry • EMC 3325 • ©2005 by Evan-Moor Corp.

Name _____

Understanding the Poem

Read each question and choose the best answer. You may wish to reread
"Tuen Ng—The Dragon Boat Races" as you work.

1. This poem tells about a race between _____.
   Ⓐ dragon-racers in a fairy tale
   Ⓑ two dragons that turned into boats
   Ⓒ boats that are decorated like dragons
   Ⓓ sea creatures that are best described as dragons

2. The "air is hushed" at the beginning of the poem because _____.
   Ⓐ a storm is on its way
   Ⓑ the waking beast is stretching
   Ⓒ the dragon has not yet appeared
   Ⓓ people are waiting for the race to start

3. The dragon's "wings" are really _____.
   Ⓐ paddles
   Ⓑ waves
   Ⓒ flags
   Ⓓ sails

4. The Dragon Boat Races _____.
   Ⓐ are loud from beginning to end
   Ⓑ begin at dawn and end at sunset
   Ⓒ start on land but end in the water
   Ⓓ start quietly and end with lots of noise

5. In general, this festival sounds like it is _____.
   Ⓐ a serious occasion
   Ⓑ fun and exciting
   Ⓒ not really a competition at all
   Ⓓ a time for giving and receiving

Understanding the Poem

Study these definitions before you do the exercises.

Simile A comparison between two things that uses the words *like* or *as*.
Example: *The river wound through the valley like a blue ribbon.* The river is compared to a ribbon, using the word *like*.

Metaphor The comparison of two things that have similar qualities.
Example: *The branches of the tree scratched my window with its claws.* The tree is being compared to a cat.

Personification The giving of human qualities to an animal, object, place, or idea.
Example: *New York City never goes to sleep.* The city is being described as if it were a living human being.

Read each of these lines from the poem. Write *S*, *M*, or *P* to show if it is an example of a simile, a metaphor, or personification. Then tell what is being compared. Follow the example.

1. __P__ The air is hushed round waiting boats;

   __The air is compared to a living, breathing human being.__

2. _____ Slowly paddles lift above the dragon-prows like giant wing-bones

   _____

3. _____ Fish scatter in dismay

   _____

4. _____ Wings dip, whip water into waves;

   _____

5. _____ waves rise like flames,

   _____

6. _____ flags tug at their fetters,

   _____

7. _____ And all around, like pumping, thumping dragon-hearts,
      the pounding gongs, the beating drum.

   _____

 Read and Understand Poetry • EMC 3325 • ©2005 by Evan-Moor Corp.

Accent See "Stressed Syllables"

Acrostic *(uh-CROSS-tick)*

In an *acrostic* poem, a word or short message is spelled out vertically using the first letter of each line. The hidden message in an acrostic is always related to the theme or main idea of the poem, as in this example from a poem about the Jewish New Year, Rosh Hashanah.

Example:
R enewal
O f
S pirit
H ealing
from "New Year Prayer" by Sarita Chávez Silverman

Alignment *(uh-LINE-mint)*

The way the words are arranged in the lines of a poem is called *alignment*. In the stanza shown in this example, all of the lines except for the last one are set centered. The last line is set off to the right. The poet may be calling special attention to the word *listening* by using this alignment.

Example:
"It's in there, sleeping,"
Don Luis says and winks.
He knows I want to feel
the animal asleep in a piece of wood,
like he does
turning it this way and that
listening.
from "The Purple Snake" by Pat Mora

Alliteration *(uh-lih-tuh-RAY-shun)*

When several words that begin with the same sound are next to each other or close together, it is called *alliteration*. In this example, the repetition of the beginning *b* creates alliteration. The effect is strengthened by the *b*'s in the middle of some words.

Example:
I bubble into eddying bays,
I babble on the pebbles.
from "The Brook" by Alfred, Lord Tennyson

Assonance *(ASS-uh-nance)*

When the same vowel sound is repeated in words that are next to each other or close together, it is called *assonance*. Assonance can make poetry more musical, and it can also make it easier to learn by heart. In this example, the words *bright, light, night, drive,* and *time* create assonance.

Example:
Bright blazing light,
burning up the night
drive the dark and cold away
make the night-time bright as day
from "Diwali" by David Harmer

Atmosphere *(AT-muss-fear)*

A poet uses words to help readers "see" the setting in a poem. It may be a still, quiet place or a busy, noisy place. In describing the setting, a poet creates an *atmosphere*. In this example, the poet uses just eighteen words to create a specific atmosphere.

Example:
Night from a railroad car window
Is a great, dark, soft thing
Broken across with slashes of light.
"Window" by Carl Sandburg

Ballad

A *ballad* is a song or poem that tells a story. Most ballads are written in *quatrains*, or four-line stanzas, with patterns of rhyme that help make them easier to recite or sing by heart. Ballads are among the earliest forms of poetry, and many continue to be passed along by word of mouth in what is called the *oral tradition*.

Example: Come all you rounders if you want to hear
                        A story 'bout a brave engineer,
                        Casey Jones was the rounder's name
                        'Twas on the Illinois Central that he won his fame.

from "The Ballad of Casey Jones" by Wallace Saunders

Capitalization

The rules for using capital letters and punctuation marks are not always strictly followed in poetry. Some poets choose not to follow them at all. In this example, though, the poet has used capital letters on words that don't require them. This was probably done to emphasize the silly nature of this limerick.

Example:

There was an Old Man in a boat,
Who said, "I'm afloat! I'm afloat!"
When they said, "No! you ain't!"
He was ready to faint,
That unhappy Old Man in a boat.

Limerick 15 from The Book of Nonsense by Edward Lear

Colloquial Language *(kuh-LOW-kwee-ul)*

Informal language and vocabulary that is part of everyday speech is referred to as *colloquial language.* Colloquial expressions include slang and familiar expressions. They are often used when a poet wants to reach simple, "regular" people or to show that they are speaking in a poem. In this example, the poet has replaced the words *blowing* and *growing* with colloquialisms.

Example:

It sets the sand a-blowing,
And the blackberries a-growing.

from "What's the Railroad to Me?" by Henry David Thoreau

Consonance

The repetition of consonant sounds at the end of words is called *consonance*. Poets use consonance to help create a musical quality in their poetry or to emphasize a particular sound. In this example, the words *trail* and *hill* create consonance.

Example:

When I walk the river trail
the ground grabs every step
and makes me pay for every hill,

from "Skating the River Trail" by Linda Armstrong

Contraction

When poets use a particular pattern of meter, or rhythm, they may sometimes need to shorten a word so that it fits the pattern. One way to shorten a word is to take out a syllable, replacing the missing letter or letters with an apostrophe. This creates a *contraction*, or shortened word. In this example, however, the contraction does not change the number of syllables. It is one of the ways that Walt Whitman experimented with words and language in his poetry.

Example: On a flat road runs the well-train'd runner;
                        He is lean and sinewy, with muscular legs;
                        He is thinly clothed—he leans forward as he runs,
                        With lightly closed fists, and arms partially rais'd.

"The Runner" by Walt Whitman

Dialog

When two or more characters have a conversation, it is called a *dialog*. When dialog is included in poetry, some poets follow the same rules of punctuation used for writing dialog in prose. Some poets do not. In this example, each speaker's words are in separate stanzas. Italic type is used for the mother's words.

Example:

When I grow up,
I want to be a doctor.

M'ija, you will patch scraped knees and wipe away children's tears.

from "Growing Up"
by Liz Ann Báez Aguilar

Free Verse

When a poem is written without a pattern of rhyme, meter, or line length, it is called *free verse*. Poets use words and images to help make free verse feel different from regular sentences, or *prose*.

Example:

Your laugh peels apples
and stirs their cinnamon bubblings,
then opens a book and pulls me
onto your lap.

from "Song to Mothers"
by Pat Mora

Haiku *(hi-KOO)*

Haiku is a form of poetry that first began in Japan in the 1700s. A haiku always has three lines. The first and third lines have five syllables, and the second line has seven. A traditional haiku focuses on an image in nature. Most haiku present a closeup look at a single detail.

Example:

Daddy's voice thunders
he shoots a lightning jumpshot
through a sweaty storm

"Lightning Jumpshot"
by Michael Burgess

Imagery *(IH-muh-jree)*

We call the words used by writers to help readers make pictures in their mind *imagery*. Notice how the poet's imagery in this example helps you make a mental picture of the runaway slave.

Example: The runaway slave came to my house and stopt outside,
I heard his motions crackling the twigs of the woodpile,
Through the swung half-door of the kitchen I saw him limpsy and weak,

from "The Runaway Slave" by Walt Whitman

Invented Words

Invented words are made up by the poet. You can usually guess what they mean by seeing how they fit with the other words in the poem. What kind of weapon is a "vorpal sword"? What sort of enemy is a "manxome foe"? What might a "Tumtum tree" be? You'll have to use your imagination.

Example:

He took his vorpal sword in hand:
Long time the manxome foe he sought—
So rested he by the Tumtum tree,
And stood awhile in thought.

from "Jabberwocky"
by Lewis Carroll

Limerick *(LIH-muh-rick)*

Limericks are silly or nonsensical rhymes that follow a very specific rhyme scheme. Limericks always have five lines. The first, second, and fifth lines always rhyme. The third and fourth lines also rhyme. Limericks always follow the same pattern of meter, or rhythm, as you'll find in this limerick.

Example:

There was a Young Lady of Clare,
Who was sadly pursued by a bear;
When she found she was tired,
She abruptly expired
That unfortunate Lady of Clare.

Limerick 112 from The Book of Nonsense
by Edward Lear

Lyrics (LIH-rix)

When the words of a poem are set to music and sung, they are called *lyrics*. Sometimes, the words and the music are created separately and combined later. Sometimes, the words and music are created at the same time. These lyrics are from a traditional sea shanty sung by sailors.

Example: 'Twas Friday morn when we set sail,
And we had not got far from land,
When the Captain, he spied a lovely mermaid,
With a comb and a glass in her hand.

from "The Mermaid," Traditional

Metaphor (MET-uh-for)

A *metaphor* compares two things by presenting them as being almost identical. For example, a metaphor that compares snow to a white blanket would read: *The snow is a white blanket.* In this example, laughter is compared to a "green song."

Example:

Your laugh is a green song,
canción verde,
that branches
through our house,

from "Song to Mothers"
by Pat Mora

Meter (MEE-tur)

A regular pattern of rhythm is called *meter*. Writing made up of sentences that use meter is called *verse*. Writing made up of sentences that do <u>not</u> use meter is called *prose*. To feel the meter in this example, clap or tap for each syllable.

Example:

With bleeding back, from tyrant's lash,
A fleet-foot slave has sped,
All frantic, past his humble hut,
And seeks the wood instead.

from "The Fugitive"
by Priscilla Jane Thompson

Narrative Verse

Narrative verse tells a story, or narrates. The difference between a narrative poem and a prose story is that the narrative poem is told in verse, so it rhymes.

Example: Listen, my children, and you shall hear
Of the midnight ride of Paul Revere,

from "The Landlord's Tale: Paul Revere's Ride" by Henry Wadsworth Longfellow

Nonsense Poems

Nonsense poems are silly rhymes that don't always make sense. Their purpose is to entertain the reader with the sound of the words and the amusing images used by the poet.

Example:

There was an Old Man of the Dee
Who was sadly annoyed by a flea;
When he said, "I will scratch it,"
They gave him a hatchet,
Which grieved that Old Man of the Dee.

Limerick 65 from **The Book of Nonsense**
by Edward Lear

Ode

A poem that uses exalted, or elevated, language to celebrate a particular subject is called an *ode*. Odes are usually written using stanzas and may be quite long. They may deal with a serious subject or be a thoughtful meditation on a topic. In this case, the poet looks at the effects of slavery on African American men. Altogether, this ode has fifteen stanzas.

Example:

Sometimes, a friendly, fellow-slave,
Chance, spying where he hid,
At night would bring his coarse, rough, fare,
And God-speed warmly bid.

from "The Fugitive"
by Priscilla Jane Thompson

Onomatopoeia *(aw-nuh-mah-tuh-PEE-uh)*

When a word sounds like the noise or sound that it stands for, it is called *onomatopoeia*. *Buzz* and *sizzle* are examples of onomatopoeia. In this example, the poet uses onomatopoeia to evoke the sounds of sheep and birds.

Example:

He heard the bleating of the flock,
And the twitter of birds among the trees,

from "The Landlord's Tale: Paul Revere's Ride"
by Henry Wadsworth Longfellow

Personification *(per-sawn-uh-fuh-KAY-shun)*

When a writer describes something that is not human as having qualities or capabilities that are human, it is called *personification*. In this example, the poet describes flags as if they have human feelings.

Example:

Above, flags tug at their fetters,
desperate to join the fun.

from "Tuen Ng—The Dragon Boat Races"
by Judith Nicholls

Quatrain *(KWAH-trane)*

A stanza made up of four rhyming lines is called a *quatrain*. Ballads are usually written using quatrains, as in this example.

Example: They pulled out of Memphis nearly two hours late,
Soon they were speeding at a terrible rate.
And the people knew by the whistle's moan
That the man at the throttle was Casey Jones.

from "The Ballad of Casey Jones" by Wallace Saunders

Refrain *(ree-FRANE)*

A *refrain* is a group of lines that are repeated two or more times in a poem. When song lyrics include a refrain, it is called a *chorus*. In Tennyson's "The Brook," the following refrain is repeated at the end of four different stanzas.

Example:

For men may come and men may go,
But I go on for ever.

from "The Brook"
by Alfred, Lord Tennyson

Repetition *(reh-peh-TIH-shun)*

When a poet uses the same word or words more than once in a line or in a poem, it is called *repetition*. Repetition can be used to emphasize a word or an idea in a poem. Repetition can also be used to create special sounds or rhythms in a poem.

Example:

Bright blazing light,
burning up the night
drive the dark and cold away
make the night-time bright as day
bright blazing light
beautiful sight

from "Diwali"
by David Harmer

Rhyming Verse

When words end with the same sound, we say they *rhyme*. Poetry with a pattern of rhyme is called *rhyming verse*. Rhyming words help make their writing sound different from prose. Rhyming words are usually placed at the end of a line in a poem. In this example, the first and third lines rhyme and the second and fourth lines rhyme, so we can show this rhyme scheme as *abab*.

Example:

And here and there a foamy flake
Upon me, as I travel
With many a silvery waterbreak
Above the golden gravel,

from "The Brook"
by Alfred, Lord Tennyson

Simile (SIH-muh-lee)

A *simile* compares one thing to another using the word *like* or *as*. In this example, the poet compares oars, or paddles, to the huge wings of a beast.

Example:

Slowly paddles lift
above the dragon-prows
like giant wing-bones
from a waking beast,

*from "Tuen Ng—The Dragon Boat Races"
by Judith Nicholls*

Sonnet (SAWE-net)

A *sonnet* has fourteen lines and follows a regular rhyme scheme. In the sonnet "The New Colossus" (see page 109), the rhyme scheme is made of two parts. The first eight lines, called an octave, has an *abbaabba* pattern. The last six lines, called a sestet, has a *cdcdcd* rhyme scheme.

Stanza (STAN-zuh)

A stanza is a group of lines in a poem. Usually, the lines in a stanza are related to each other in the same way that the sentences of a paragraph "go together."

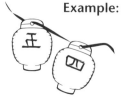

Example: It's New Year's Day
in China Town,
another year
is counted down. ⌉1

Fireworks shoot
showers of light
lanterns wave,
burning bright. ⌉2

from "Chinese New Year in China Town" by Andrew Collett

Stressed Syllables

Rhyming verse usually has meter, or a pattern of rhythm. Poets use the natural pattern of accented, or stressed, syllables in the words they choose to help set the poem's rhythm. In the example at right, the syllables where the accent, or stress, falls appear in the darker boldface type.

Example:

It's **New** Year's **Day**
in **Chi**na **Town**,
a**noth**er **year**
is **count**ed **down**.

*from "Chinese New Year in China Town"
by Andrew Collett*

Traditional Poetry

The authors of *traditional poetry* are unknown. Traditional poems have been recited and passed down from one generation to the next. Often, these poems were recited for years before anyone wrote them down. There are often several different versions of traditional poems. This traditional ballad is hundreds of years old.

Example: Then three times 'round went our gallant ship,
And three times 'round went she,
And the third time that she went 'round
She sank to the bottom of the sea.

from "The Mermaid," Traditional

Word Order

In English, basic sentence structure begins with a subject, followed by a verb and a complement. Poets often change this typical *word order* to achieve a particular rhyme scheme or to add musicality to their poetry. In this example, Shakespeare has changed the usual order of "his bones are made of coral."

Example:

Full fathom five thy father lies.
Of his bones are coral made;

*from "Full Fathom Five"
by William Shakespeare*

Liz Ann Báez Aguilar

Liz Ann Báez Aguilar is a native of San Antonio, Texas, where she teaches English at San Antonio College. She also enjoys spending time with her family, doing community service work, and writing. Her stories have appeared in *Kaleidoscope* and other journals. Ms. Aguilar encourages young people to discover the power of words and their capacity to express joy and beauty.

Francisco X. Alarcón

Francisco X. Alarcón considers himself a poet first, then a teacher. He grew up in both the United States and Mexico, and is proud to be bilingual and bicultural. Mr. Alarcón is committed to helping Latinos develop strong reading and writing skills in both of their languages, and now works directing the Spanish for Native Speakers Program at the University of California at Davis. He is the author of seven books of poetry for young people and adults, and has coauthored several textbooks for Spanish speakers.

Linda Armstrong

Linda Armstrong started composing verses before she could write. She remembers sitting in the back seat of the family car inventing rhyming chants during family outings. She wrote poems on scraps of paper all through school, and she continued to write after graduating from college with a degree in English. Her first published poems appeared in *The National Anthology of High School Poetry,* and a collection of her poetry, *Early Tigers,* was published in 1995.

Michael Burgess

Michael Burgess is a writer and actor who was born and raised in South Carolina. "Lightning Jumpshot" is Mr. Burgess's first published poem for children.

Lewis Carroll

Lewis Carroll was the pen name of Charles Lutwidge Dodgson, who lived in England from 1832 to 1898, during the reign of Queen Victoria. He was an amateur magician and taught math by profession. Today, however, he is most famous as the author of *Alice's Adventures in Wonderland.* His poetry and stories are characterized by logic and puzzles. His themes are typically whimsical.

Andrew Collett

Andrew Collett began writing poetry as a teacher. Since then, over one hundred of his poems have been published. He now writes and performs his poetry in schools across Great Britain.

David Harmer

David Harmer is a teacher. Many of his stories and poems for children and adults have appeared in a wide variety of collections, anthologies, and magazines. He also visits schools to help children and teachers with creative writing.

Emma Lazarus

Emma Lazarus was born into a prominent Jewish family in New York City. She wrote mostly about Jewish history and cultural life. In 1883, she wrote "The New Colossus" for an auction to help raise funds for the pedestal for the Statue of Liberty. The poem was added to the pedestal in 1901, three years after her death.

Edward Lear

Edward Lear (1812–1888) lived in England during the reign of Queen Victoria. He was best known during his lifetime as an illustrator, focusing especially on scientific depictions of birds and other wildlife. Since his death, however, he has become known mainly for mastering the whimsical form known as the limerick, as well as for his other humorous poems. While the subject and form of his works vary, nearly all are characterized by an irreverent view of the world. Lear poked fun at everything, including himself.

Henry Wadsworth Longfellow

Henry Wadsworth Longfellow lived from 1807 to 1882. He was one of America's best-loved poets. His poetry is easily understood, with simple, familiar themes. Most people enjoy the patterns of rhythm and rhyme in his poems. He was one of the first artists to use American history, culture, landscape, and traditions as a focus in his art.

Pat Mora

Pat Mora is an award-winning author of poetry, nonfiction, and children's books. She has published over 20 books for young readers, and often speaks at schools and conferences about writing and multicultural education. A native of El Paso, Texas, she now divides her time between Santa Fe, New Mexico, and Cincinnati, Ohio.

Judith Nicholls

Judith Nicholls is a British poet who has written and compiled nearly 40 books, and her poems can be found in over 300 anthologies. She now lives in an ancient cottage in a Wiltshire churchyard in England.

Carl Sandburg

Carl Sandburg was born to Swedish immigrant parents in Galesburg, Illinois, in 1878. His father worked as a blacksmith's helper for the railroad. Carl left school after eighth grade and worked for ten years before traveling for a year as a hobo. This experience made a lasting impression on him, and he developed deep admiration for American workers. Sandburg eventually finished college and began to work in journalism. With the publication of *Chicago Poems* in 1914, he began a long career as a poet, children's book author, and noted biographer of Abraham Lincoln. Sandburg has been recognized as one of the most distinguished American poets of the 20th century and was awarded the Pulitzer Prize for both poetry and biography.

Wallace Saunders

Wallace Saunders was an engine wiper in the railroad shop in Canton, Mississippi. He was a friend of Casey Jones, the engineer of the "Cannonball Special," the train that was made famous when it was destroyed in a spectacular wreck. When the train wreck occurred, Saunders wrote this ballad, which he sang and played around Canton. In 1902, the song was published and became a national hit, but others were given credit for the words and music. The song made Casey Jones a legend, but Wallace Saunders never made a dime from it.

William Shakespeare

William Shakespeare is generally considered the greatest playwright the world has ever known. He is equally famous for his sonnets, and is also recognized as the greatest poet in the English-speaking world. He lived and wrote in 17th century England. The subject matter of his poetry ranges across the breadth of the imagination. It is his mastery of the English language that sets Shakespeare at a level above all other poets.

Sarita Chávez Silverman

Sarita Chávez Silverman was awarded the Cowell Translation Prize in 1978 for her translation of poetry by Federico García Lorca. In 1996, one of her children's books was recognized as a commended title by the jury of the Americas Award for Children's Literature. Ms. Silverman works in curriculum development for young learners and in second-language instruction. Her creative interests reflect her mixed Jewish and Latino heritage.

Alfred, Lord Tennyson

Alfred Tennyson (1809–1892) was a British poet laureate who was one of the most important English poets during the reign of Queen Victoria. He started writing poetry at the age of eight, and had almost completed a play written in blank verse by age fourteen. Queen Victoria gave Tennyson the title "Lord" in 1884.

Priscilla Jane Thompson

Priscilla Jane Thompson was an African American who wrote poetry in the late 19th and early 20th centuries. She wanted to use her poetry to present a realistic picture of African Americans, to show qualities that were often ignored. "The Fugitive" shows how successful she was in portraying the patience, fortitude, and forbearance of her people.

Henry David Thoreau

Henry David Thoreau was an American writer, philosopher, and naturalist who lived and wrote in the early 19th century. A major portion of his time was devoted to the study of nature. From 1845 until 1847, he lived in a primitive hut on the shores of Walden Pond in Massachusetts. His writing style initially seems plain and direct, but his witty similes, puns, and turns on conventional proverbs reveal a subtle, more complex depth.

Jennifer Trujillo

Jennifer Trujillo, a writer of Venezuelan descent, was raised in her birthplace, Denver, Colorado, and in Caracas, Venezuela. A winner of the *Latina* magazine essay contest, Trujillo teaches at Fort Lewis College in Durango and at the Navajo Indian Reservation in Cortez, Colorado.

Walt Whitman

Walt Whitman is considered one of the greatest American poets of the 19th century. His collection of poems, *Leaves of Grass,* is considered one of the world's major literary works. It marked a revolutionary development in poetry. Whitman's use of free verse and rhythmic innovations were in sharp contrast to the rigid rhyming and structural patterns which had been thought to be essential for poetic expression prior to that time.

My Read & Understand

Poetry
Anthology

This book belongs to:

_____

Online Resources

The Academy of American Poets: http://www.poets.org

This comprehensive Web site includes over 1,400 poems, 500 poet biographies, and 100 audio clips of 20th- and 21st-century poets reading their own works (e.g., Gwendolyn Brooks, E. E. Cummings, Robert Frost, Langston Hughes, William Carlos Williams, and others). This site also includes the following:

- the Online Poetry Classroom, with free access to poetry curriculum units and other educational resources for teachers
- the National Poetry Almanac and Calendar, which track poetry-related events nationwide throughout the year
- information on National Poetry Month (April)

Lee & Low Books: http://www.leeandlow.com

Publishers of multicultural literature for children, Lee & Low Books has excellent poetry-related material on the Poetry Power page of their Web site. You'll find the following:

- ideas for bringing poetry into the classroom, by poet Pat Mora and literacy educator Regie Routman
- information on additional resources for incorporating poetry into primary classrooms
- digital movies of contemporary poets of color reading their works, including Tony Medina reading "My Grandmother Had One Good Coat" (included in *Read and Understand Poetry, Grades 5–6*) and Pat Mora reading "Song to Mothers" (included in *Read and Understand Poetry, Grades 2–3*).

Audio Resources

In Their Own Voices—A Century of Recorded Poetry, ©1996, WEA/Atlantic/Rhino

This four-CD boxed set includes 122 poems recorded by their authors, including Robert Frost, Walt Whitman, William Carlos Williams (reading "The Red Wheelbarrow," included in *Read and Understand Poetry, Grades 5–6*), and contemporary poets such as Maya Angelou, Lucille Clifton, Gary Snyder, Carmen Tafolla, and others. In compiling this impressive collection, poetry historian and recording producer Rebekah Presson drew from the Library of Congress archives, poets' personal archives, and recordings made on her 1980s radio show, *New Letters on the Air*. The collection also includes a printed booklet with additional information. Check your public library for a copy of this excellent collection.

The Writer's Almanac®

This is a short program (about five minutes in length) of poetry and history hosted by Garrison Keillor, heard daily on public radio stations. Check their Web site at http:writersalmanac.publicradio.org for local station listings. The Web site also has searchable archives.

Print Resources

Writing Poetry with Children by Jo Ellen Moore, ©1999 by Evan-Moor Corporation

Step-by-step lessons provide guidance for introducing a variety of poetic forms and supporting primary-age students in producing original poetry in each form.

Teaching 10 Fabulous Forms of Poetry by Paul Janeczko, ©2000 by Scholastic

Geared for intermediate grades (4–8), this volume introduces 10 poetic forms and supports students in planning and writing original poetry in each form.

See also the many fine poetry resource books listed on the Web sites noted above.

Song to Mothers - Page 8
1. C—a small child
2. B—laughter
3. C—speaks another language besides English
4. D—spends a lot of time with her children
5. C—bubbles in cooking apples

Page 9
1. a tree, yellow flowers, warm honey
2. peels apples, stirs cinnamon, opens a book, pulls a child onto her lap, kisses her children, puts the children to bed
3. metaphor
4. Answers will vary.
5. Answers will vary.

My Grandma Is Like a Flowering Cactus
Page 12
1. C—autumn
2. D—covered with thorns
3. A—good to eat
4. B—a type of cactus fruit
5. D—is sweet, just like the fruit of a prickly pear

Page 13
1. • The time of year when prickly pears become ripe
   • How the poet's grandma harvests prickly pears—the tools she uses and the way that she sings songs
   • He tells how his grandma winks at him while she's peeling the prickly pears. That shows it's special to him.
2. • "picks the prickly pears"
   • "peels prickly pears" and "delicacies of the desert"
   • "favorite fruits by far"
   • Answers will vary. Examples could be *wriggly, writhing rattlesnakes; smooth, soft sand; rabbits and roadrunners.*

The Race - Page 17
1. D—Abuela, the poet's grandmother
2. B—cowboy
3. A—a rose
4. C—one
5. D—the first woman to ever win this race

Page 18
Stanzas 1–3
Abuela and her horse Fina love to ride around the mountain. Great-grandma wants to put a stop to it, but then they hear about a race in town.

Stanzas 4 and 5
Abuela and Fina decide to enter the race, even though it's supposed to be for men.

Stanzas 6–8
Abuela and Fina win the race way ahead of all the others.

The Crocodile - Page 22
1. A—Nile River
2. B—meat eaters
3. B—does
4. C—setting a trap
5. A—make fun of another poem

Page 23
1. They are both about animals. They show how the animal gets what it needs for food.

2. The poem about the bee is trying to show that it's good to work hard. The other one is about how lazy the crocodile is. It doesn't seem to have a "message" at all.
3. A parody must be a kind of copy. It's a poem that copies another kind of poem, but not in a serious way. It copies the poem to make fun of it.

Selections from *The Book of Nonsense*
Page 26
1. B—giggle at something silly
2. B—was sinking
3. B—He hurt himself with the hatchet.
4. A—suddenly died
5. C—She was caught by the bear.

Page 27
1. <u>There was</u> an Old Man in a boat,
   <u>Who</u> said, "I'm afloat! I'm afloat!"
   <u>When</u> they said, "No! you ain't!"
   He was ready to faint,
   That unhappy Old Man in a boat.
2. *aabba*
3. Limericks will vary.

Jabberwocky - Page 30
1. B—a horrible monster
2. A—Jubjub
3. C—Tumtum tree
4. C—Hip, hip, hooray!
5. B—knights and dragons

Page 31
Answers may vary. If not as shown here, ask students to replace nonsense words with familiar words to support their answers.

1.
Bandersnatch <u>n</u>	mome <u>n</u>
borogove <u>n</u>	outgrabe <u>v</u>
burbled <u>v</u>	rath <u>v</u>
frabjous <u>a</u>	slithy <u>a</u>
galumphing <u>v</u>	toves <u>n</u>
gimble <u>v</u>	tulgey <u>a</u>
Jabberwock <u>n</u>	uffish <u>a</u>
Jubjub <u>n</u>	vorpal <u>a</u>
manxome <u>a</u>	wabe <u>n</u>
mimsy <u>a</u>	whiffling <u>v</u>

2. Answers will vary.

The Runner - Page 35
1. A—while he is running
2. C—runs on a regular basis
3. B—overweight
4. D—muscles
5. A—paint a picture

Page 36
1. well-train'd, lean, sinewy, muscular, thinly clothed
2. lightly closed, partially rais'd
3. Possible answers:

Jockey	Weight lifter	Ballerina	Boxer
• light • small body • leaning forward in the saddle • gripping his riding crop tightly	• bulging muscles • powerful shoulders • legs thick as tree trunks • glistening with sweat • straining with all his might	• slender and graceful • rising up on her toes • powerful legs • sculptured muscles	• rippling muscles • bulging biceps • bruised cheekbone • sweat dripping from his brow

4. Answers will vary.

Lightning Jumpshot - Page 39
1. D—watching his father play basketball
2. A—quick and forceful
3. B—a good player
4. C—the players on the other team
5. A—admires

Page 40
2.

Words That Start with *s* Sound	Words That Start with *sh* Sound	Words That End with *s* Sound	Words That End with *z* Sound
scary	shake	curse	choose
see	shampoo	face	freeze
sidewalk	shiver	ice	knees
skateboard	sugar	pants	legs
skeleton	sure	worse	was

3. Answers will vary. Examples might include:
   - It would be scary to see a skeleton skateboard on a sidewalk.
   - I sure did shake and shiver when I shampooed my hair with sugar.
   - My face hitting the ice hurt worse than shinsplints, for sure.
   - Would you choose to freeze your legs if you knew it was good for your knees?

Skating the River Trail - Page 43
1. A—along a river
2. C—She has to work hard to get up the hill.
3. C—feels like she can fly
4. D—Carefully but smoothly move each foot forward one at a time.
5. B—strong

Page 44
1. the *ground grabs every step* and *makes me pay* for every hill
2. Answers will vary, but should convey the idea that she's showing that she feels slow and heavy when she's walking along the trail.
3. Answers will vary.

I Hear America Singing - Page 48
1. C—workers and their songs
2. B—blacksmith
3. D—calculating
4. A—lunch break
5. A—seem to like their jobs

Page 49
1. mechanics, carpenter, mason, boatman, deckhand, shoemaker, hatter, wood-cutter, ploughboy, housewife, seamstress, washing woman
2. Answers will vary.
3. Answers will vary.

The Village Blacksmith - Page 53
1. C—a small town a long time ago
2. A—works with his hands
3. C—working through good times and bad times
4. B—honesty and hard work
5. B—is a good model for the community

Page 54
1. Circled:
   rot/taught
   sea/comedy
   boys/noise
   eyes/rise
   floor/core

   Crossed Out:
   money/rely
   choice/spice
   voice/views
   goes/does
   drought/thought
2. Answers will vary.
3. Answers will vary.

Purple Snake - Page 57
1. D—a sculptor
2. D—It hasn't been carved yet.
3. B—gently touches
4. C—a green bull and a red frog
5. A—fanciful

Page 58
1. Writings will vary.
2. Writings will vary.

Growing Up - Page 61
1. B—a dialog
2. C—a mother and daughter
3. B—builds houses
4. C—do whatever she wants
5. B—is caring, loving, and wise

Page 62
Answers will vary.

Night Train - Page 66
1. B—during a train trip
2. A—late at night
3. D—a great, dark, soft thing
4. D—the world would be better if more people acted kindly
5. C—traveling alone

Page 67
1. Answers will vary.
2. Answers will vary.
3. Answers will vary. Examples may include highways, dark woods, city lights, empty platforms.
4. Answers will vary. Examples may include people watching movies on their DVD players, sleeping babies, dim lights, wrappers stuffed between the seats.
5. Answers will vary. Examples may include the clickety-clack of the train, people talking, somebody snoring, music coming from a neighbor's headset.
6. Answers will vary. Examples may include stale coffee, perfume and cologne, dusty cushions.
7. Answers will vary. Examples: thin blanket around my shoulders, head resting on a small pillow, elbows on plastic armrest.
8. Answers will vary.
9. Poems will vary.

What's the Railroad to Me? - Page 70
1. D—the countryside
2. A—city
3. C—a small valley
4. B—a mound of earth
5. C—just part of the landscape

Page 71
1. Answers will vary. Possible answers may be: In his poem, he sounds like he doesn't think they were very important. He describes the railroad as a place for blackberries to grow and for swallows to make their nests. In reality, he probably didn't think railroads were so innocent. He seems like the kind of person who didn't like modern technology.
2. Answers will vary.
3. Trains shortened travel times. They allowed people to visit friends and relatives in faraway places. Business people could set up new businesses more easily, too.
4. Answers will vary. Possible responses could be: The Internet allows goods and services to be traded faster than ever before, just as trains did in the nineteenth century. They both speeded up communication, too.
5. Answers will vary. Some students may think that the Internet is a way to keep in touch with friends. Others will say it is a great tool for learning and getting information. Still others may simply enjoy it as a form of entertainment.

The Ballad of Casey Jones - Page 75

1. D—a railroad line
2. A—was tired
3. D—ramming into a caboose on the main line
4. B—died and went to heaven
5. A—people still admired Casey

Page 76

1. _6_ Another train is on the main line.

   _3_ Casey agrees, as long as he can use his own engine and take Sim Webb with him.

   _9_ The great engineer, Casey Jones, is buried in Jackson, Tennessee.

   _5_ The Cannonball nears Vaughn at about 4 o'clock in the morning.

   _7_ Casey tells Webb to jump out of the Cannonball, and he does.

   _8_ The Cannonball crashes, and Casey Jones is killed.

   _2_ The engine foreman tells Casey that he has to take over for Joe Lewis.

   _1_ The Number Four train arrives in Memphis.

   _4_ To make up for lost time, Casey made the Cannonball Special go at full speed.

2. This is a sample answer:
   Late one night, the Number Four train arrived in Memphis. Casey Jones was the engineer. When he pulled into the station, the foreman told him that he had to take over for Joe Lewis, another engineer. Casey agreed, but he wanted to use his own engine and take Sim Webb with him. Sim was Casey's personal fireman. To make up for lost time, Casey made the Cannonball Special go at full speed. It got to Vaughn at about 4 o'clock in the morning. Lo and behold, another train was on the main line. Casey told Webb to jump, and he did. Unfortunately, the Cannonball crashed, and Casey was killed.

The Brook - Page 81

1. B—until it joins a river
2. B—a farmhouse
3. D—sound it makes as it washes over rocks and stones
4. C—slows down in some places
5. B—will go on no matter what people do

Page 82

1. Answers will vary, but may include some of the following:

Water		Fire		Wind	
Sounds	Movement	Sounds	Movement	Sounds	Movement
bicker down chatter bubble babble murmur	sudden sally sparkle out hurry down wind about in and out steal by slide move skip glance	crackle pop hiss	leap shoot out settle spread jump	whistle moan sing groan howl	blow gust sweep

2. Answers will vary.
3. Answers will vary.
4. Answers will vary.

The Mermaid - Page 85

1. D—after coming across a mermaid
2. A—a mirror
3. A—He knew he was going to die.
4. B—the pilot
5. C—final words before they die

Page 86

1. Answers will vary. Examples:
   <u>What the Captain felt:</u> "I'm going to miss my wife."
   <u>What the Cook felt:</u> "I wish I never got on this ship. It wasn't worth it. I'm not a sailor. All I want to do is be a cook."
   <u>What the Cabin-boy felt:</u> "Nobody in the world really cares if I live or die. I feel so lonely."

2. Answers will vary. Examples:
   <u>Good-luck superstitions:</u> If you find a four-leaf clover, you'll have good luck; If you find a wishbone while you're eating chicken or turkey, ask somebody to help you pull it apart, but make a wish first. The person that gets the biggest part of the wishbone will have his or her wish granted.
   <u>Bad-luck superstitions:</u> If you walk under a ladder, something bad will happen. The same thing is true if a black cat walks across your path.

Full Fathom Five - Page 89

1. A—drowned
2. B—thirty feet
3. B—eyes and bones
4. D—go through
5. C—funeral service

Page 90

1. Responses will vary.
2. Responses will vary.

The Landlord's Tale: Paul Revere's Ride

Page 97

1. B—his friend's name
2. D—Paul Revere riding to warn the patriots
3. C—soldiers
4. B—Paul Revere rode all the way to Concord
5. D—frightening

Page 98

1. Answers will vary.
2. Answers will vary.
3. Answers will vary.

The Runaway Slave - Page 101

1. D—escaped and is on the run
2. A—he was weak and injured
3. C—before slavery was abolished
4. C—a rifle or shotgun
5. D—broke rules when he thought it was the right thing to do

Page 102

1. _3_ He asked the runaway to come indoors.

   _2_ The man who lived there came outside.

   _5_ The man gave the runaway some clothes and a place to sleep.

   _7_ They ate dinner together.

   _8_ After seven days, the runaway could walk once again.

   _4_ The owner of the house brought the runaway water to bathe in.

   _1_ A runaway slave stopped by a cabin in the woods.

   _9_ He continued on his way north after he was stronger.

   _6_ The man in the cabin tended to the runaway's injuries.

2. Answers will vary.

The Fugitive - Page 106

1. C—have escaped and are on the run
2. A—his own wits
3. B—Canada
4. C—worth all the risks he took
5. A—is proud of her race

Page 107

1. With bleeding back, from tyrant's **lash**,   whip
   A **fleet-foot** slave has sped,   quick

   By **devious way**, cross many a stream,   back roads
   He fiercely **pressed** that day,   continued

   And sometimes, when to hunger fierce,
   He's seem almost to **yield**,   give in
   A bird would fall into his **clutch**,   trap
   A fish would shake his reel.

Read and Understand Poetry • EMC 3325 • ©2005 by Evan-Moor Corp.

And when on reaching colder **climes**,   climate
A sheep-cote shelter made,
Or, law-abiding Yankee, stern,
Clandestinely, lent aid.   secretly

But from suspense and **thralldom** freed,   fear
His **manhood** wakes at last,   sense of pride

And **Providence**, in years that came,   good fortune
Sent blessings **rife**, his way,   in abundance

The New Colossus - Page 110
1. C—the Mother of Exiles
2. C—the Statue of Liberty
3. A—miserable
4. D—She is not impressed by them.
5. B—the uplifted hand with a torch

Page 111
1. Answers will vary.
2.

fame	**land**	**she**	**poor**
flame	stand	free	shore
name	beacon-hand	me	door
frame	command		

3. Answers will vary, but should convey the idea that the Colossus of Rhodes was more a warning symbol, whereas the Statue of Liberty is a symbol of welcome.
4. the harbor, or entry, to the U.S., the land of opportunity

Chinese New Year in China Town - Page 115
1. C—lanterns and fireworks
2. B—fireworks go off
3. C—because it's New Year's Day
4. A—good luck
5. B—a happy time

Page 116

It's Néw Year's Dáy
in Chína Tówn,
anóther yeár
is coúnted dówn.

Fíreworks shoót
shówers of líght
lánterns wáve,
búrning bríght.

Chíldren dánce
ín the crówd,
smíling fáces
cheér out loúd.

Drágons twíst
úp and dówn,
for it's Néw Year's Dáy
in Chína Tówn.

New Year Prayer - Page 119
1. C—hopes and fears
2. A—humanity
3. D—a person's spirit
4. B—building a temple
5. C—hopeful and positive

Page 120
1. rewrite—write again
   reappear—appear again
   review—view again
2. Answers will vary. Examples could include: More interpretations are possible without the punctuation.

3. harmony—a pleasing combination
   spirit—life force
   humanity—all human beings
4. healing, heart, harmony, humanity
5. all humans, human caring, compassion
6. renewal of spirit, healing heart and soul, harmony among nations and humanity

Diwali - Page 123
1. D—meditating about trouble and problems
2. C—light candles and lamps
3. D—happiness and prosperity
4. D—live together in the heavens
5. C—on windowsills

Page 124
1.

Line from Poem	Alliteration	Assonance
Bright, blazing light	✔	✔
drive the dark and cold away	✔	
make the night-time bright as day		✔
to bring us wealth, bring us love		
bright blazing light this Diwali night	✔	✔

2. Answers will vary. Examples:
   blaze: burning, blazing, fire in a barn
   drive: driving down a darkened driveway
   wealth: We are wealthy in every which way.
3. Answers will vary. Examples:
   blaze: blazing flames
   drive: driving down Highway 5
   wealth: wealth and health
4. Answers will vary. Examples:
   blaze: The barn blazed away.
   drive: Don't drink and drive, or you might die.
   wealth: Wither went my wealth?

Tuen Ng—The Dragon Boat Races - Page 127
1. C—boats that are decorated like dragons
2. D—people are waiting for the race to start
3. A—paddles
4. D—start quietly and end with lots of noise
5. B—fun and exciting

Page 128
1. _P_ The air is hushed round waiting boats;
   The air is compared to a living, breathing human being.
2. _S_ Slowly paddles lift above the dragon-prows
   like giant wing-bones
   The paddles are compared to wing-bones using the word _like_.
3. _P_ Fish scatter in dismay
   The fish are compared to people with feelings.
4. _M_ Wings dip, whip water into waves;
   The paddles are compared to wings.
5. _S_ waves rise like flames,
   Waves are compared to flames using the word _like_.
6. _P_ or _M_ flags tug at their fetters,
   Flags are described as things with hands.
7. _S_ And all around, like pumping, thumping dragon-hearts,
   the pounding gongs, the beating drum.
   Gongs and drums are compared to dragon-hearts using the word _like_.

Read and Understand Poetry • EMC 3325 • ©2005 by Evan-Moor Corp.